EARLY AMERICAN LITHOGRAPHY

Images to 1830

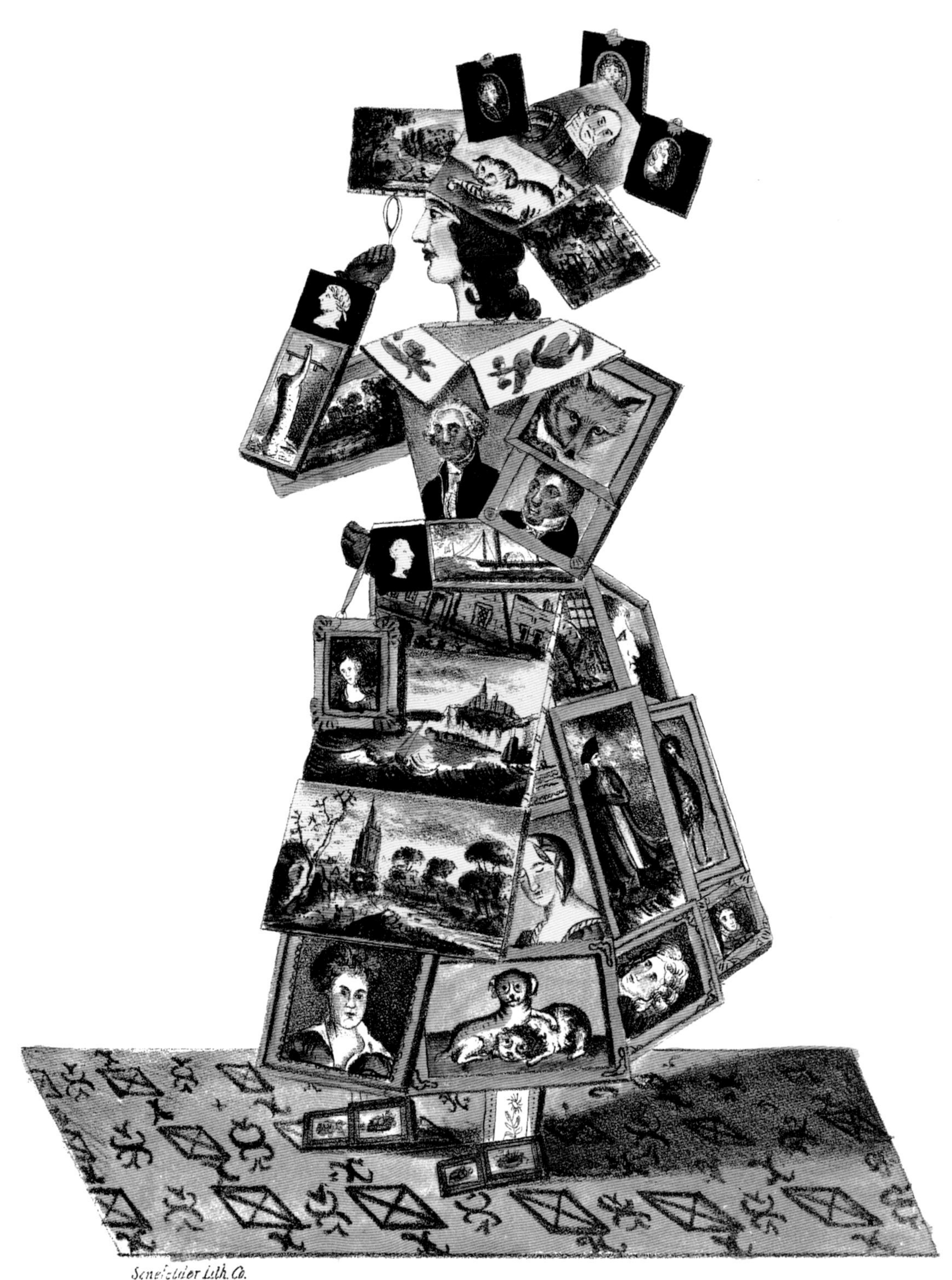

THE CONNOISSEUR.

Sold by Kettell 59 Cornhill.

EARLY AMERICAN LITHOGRAPHY

Images to 1830

by SALLY PIERCE

with CATHARINA SLAUTTERBACK

and GEORGIA BRADY BARNHILL

The Boston Athenæum BOSTON · MASSACHUSETTS

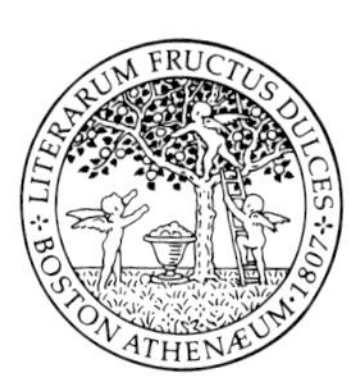

This catalogue is published on the occasion of an exhibition in the Boston Athenæum Gallery, 17 April–20 June 1997.

Library of Congress Catalogue Card Number 97-70985

ISBN 0-934552-64-9

Design & Typography by Howard I. Gralla
Printed by Hull Printing Company, Inc.
Bound by Mueller Trade Bindery

Cover and frontispiece:
Anonymous. Composite figures printed by the Senefelder Lithographic Company. Boston, ca. 1830–1831. (Cat. 77).

For CHARLES E. MASON, JR.

PREFACE AND ACKNOWLEDGMENTS

It was only a few years ago, in 1991, that the Boston Athenæum had the opportunity to present an extensive exhibition devoted to American lithography. That show, entitled *Boston Lithography: 1825–1880,* enabled us to begin to suggest the richness of the Athenæum's lithographic collections, which form an important part of our holdings dedicated to the printmaker's art.

The exhibition accompanying this catalogue is more chronologically focused, but no less ambitious. In returning to this subject on the occasion of the bicentennial of the discovery of the lithographic process by Alois Senefelder in Munich, we have been able to focus on an artistic and commercial history that is sometimes quite different from its European counterpart. The entries in *Early American Lithography: Images to 1830* are primarily drawn from the 1820s, when the lithographic process first began to flourish in the United States, but they range from the early experiments of Bass Otis in 1819 to the more polished productions of 1830.

This exhibition and its catalogue, moreover, are a collaborative effort between the Boston Athenæum and our colleagues at the American Antiquarian Society, which houses one of the other great collections of lithographic images in this country. Thirty-nine of the seventy-seven objects in the show are drawn from the collections in Worcester, and we are most grateful to Georgia Brady Barnhill, Andrew W. Mellon Curator of Graphic Arts at the American Antiquarian Society, who collaborated with the Athenæum's Sally Pierce (Curator of the Charles E. Mason, Jr., Print Room) and Catharina Slautterback, our Associate Curator, in mounting the exhibition and writing the catalogue.

By combining our resources with those of the American Antiquarian Society, we have been able to reveal the achievements of lithographic artists and printers during the formative years — the incunable period — of American lithography. The two collections overlap in a complementary fashion. The Boston Athenæum collection concentrates on Boston lithography and has particularly strong holdings of topographical views. The American Antiquarian Society collection contains lithographs printed in all of the early printmaking centers: Philadelphia, New York, Washington, and even Richmond, Virginia. The American Antiquarian Society collection contains a wide range of subject matter, with particular strengths in genre and landscape prints. Both collections are indebted to individual collectors: the American Antiquarian Society collection to Charles Henry Taylor, the Athenæum collection to Charles E. Mason, Jr., Trustee Emeritus, Honorary Curator of Prints, and benefactor of the Athenæum's Print Room. This catalogue is affectionately and appropriately dedicated to "Monk" Mason.

Charles Henry Taylor (1867–1941) was the greatest donor of pictorial materials in the history of the American Antiquarian Society. In his obituary of Taylor, Clarence S. Brigham, the Society's librarian, pointed out that "not since Isaiah Thomas has any one donor given to the Library so great a mass of historical material." Among his gifts were 15,000 stereograph views, correspondence of publishing firms, and important material on printing history, including Abel Bowen's copy of G. Engelmann's *Manuel du dessinateur lithographe* (Paris, 1822). Lithographs came in the form of separately published prints, detached book illustrations, and books and periodicals that were lithographically illustrated. Taylor, moreover, paid to have the collection arranged and indexed, and in 1922 published "Some Notes on Early American Lithography" in the *Proceedings of the American Antiquarian Society*.

As the newly appointed Director and Librarian of the Boston Athenæum, it gives me great pleasure to pay tribute to the many colleagues who have nurtured this project during the past several years. I am particularly indebted to my predecessor, Rodney Armstrong, and to my friends and colleagues Ellen Dunlap, President of the American Antiquarian Society, and Nancy Burkett, the Society's librarian. Their support of — and encouragement to — the three authors of this catalogue are greatly appreciated.

The individual entries in the catalogue are filled with citations to earlier scholars in the field, but one scholar deserves particular mention here. David Tatham's seminal article on the Pendleton shop and the artists associated with it (as well as numerous other publications) laid the groundwork for our current effort. Tatham's work legitimized American lithography, making it a subject for serious art historical research.

The authors and I are also indebted to a number of other colleagues who have assisted in the preparation of the catalogue and exhibition. Michael Wentworth (Curator of the Athenæum's art collection), Ruth Morley (Associate Director), and Ann Wadsworth (Editor of Publications) formed the advisory committee that moved the exhibition from conception to fruition. At the beginning of the project, Lauren Hewes of the American Antiquarian Society volunteered to help with the research by reading the *National Gazette and Literary Register*, a Philadelphia newspaper, to glean references to prints in general and lithography in particular. Courtney Wood, an intern in the Athenæum's Print Room, searched through the *Boston Daily Advertiser* and the *Independent Chronicle and Boston Patriot*. These citations have added significantly to the project, and we are most appreciative of Lauren and Courtney's time and effort.

Stanley Cushing, Anne Pelikan, and Barbara Hebard of the Boston Athenæum's Conservation Department, and Antiquarian Society Conservator Babette Gehnrich prepared the prints and books for exhibition. Joanne Miller, an intern in the Athenæum's Print Room, assisted with loan registration, exhibition preparation, and installation. Monica Higgins, who handles special events at the Athenæum, was in charge of receptions and related programs; Frank D'Agnello and Guillermo Fernandez of the Engineering Department prepared the gallery and assisted in the installation.

It also gives me pleasure to thank Clive Russ, who photographed the Athenæum images reproduced here, and Howard I. Gralla, who designed the catalogue with his usual intelligence and care. Photographs of Antiquarian Society prints were made by Les Gardner Photography of Sturbridge, Massachusetts.

Richard Wendorf
Director and Librarian

EARLY AMERICAN LITHOGRAPHY

Images to 1830

by SALLY PIERCE

IN CONSIDERING the introduction of lithography into America, it is helpful to review the history of the invention of the process by Alois Senefelder (1771–1834) in Munich, two hundred years ago. Senefelder's autobiographical account is in large part a litany of strained financial circumstances, technical difficulties, and inadequate public support. All of these circumstances would be repeated in the American experience of the art, which was particularly driven by commercial considerations.

By his own admission, Senefelder began his lithographic experiments in an attempt to find a cheap alternative to having his plays printed by commercial letterpress.[1] His initial discovery, involving the famous laundry list of 1796, resulted in his development of a new method of etching stone to form a relief printing surface. As Senefelder recounted the incident, he had on hand a slab of polished stone that he intended to use for practice in writing backwards. His mother, in a great rush, demanded that he make up a list of the laundry that was about to be taken away by the washer-woman, and, having no pencil or paper anywhere in the house, the distracted inventor wrote the list on the polished stone, using a greasy black ink that he had prepared for his writing practice. Some time later, continuing his original plans for the stone, he etched it using *aqua fortis,* or nitric acid, and discovered that the greasy ink acted as a resist, creating raised letters that could then be printed as from a relief plate.

Senefelder's revolutionary and enduring contribution to printmaking came two years later, in 1798, when he perfected his method of "chemical printing," based on the antipathy of grease and water. In this process, which is still used today, a greasy crayon or ink is used to draw or mark on a polished slab of limestone that has been chemically prepared. After the image has been drawn, the stone is again chemically treated, sponged with water, inked, and printed while still damp. As long as the stone is damp, the printer's ink will adhere only to the greasy marks. Unlike relief printing, where the design is raised, or intaglio printing, where the design is incised into the plate, a lithograph is printed from a level surface and is called planographic printing.

Senefelder's first contracts for the application of the new medium were for printing music. Although in his treatise on lithography, published in Munich in 1818, Senefelder fully described the range of techniques that could be used by artists working on stone, he continued to stress the utility of the process, citing, among other examples, the benefits to be gained from printing government edicts and military orders.

While Senefelder continued to explore and improve the technical aspects of lithography, other promoters, attracted by the medium's unique ability to multiply drawings directly from the artist's hand, sought to benefit from the new aesthetic possibilities. In Berlin, William Reuter (1768–1834) published *Polyautographic Drawings by Leading Berlin Artists* (1804–1808), a large, beautifully presented portfolio that is a tour de force of lithographic handling and subject matter. A similarly impressive series was undertaken in London, where Benjamin West (1738–1820), the American expatriate, and other members of the Royal Academy, contributed to the *Specimens of Polyautography* (1803–1807), published by Philip André.

In the United States, however, there was no cadre of well trained, established artists to enlist in the lithographic cause. The story of the birth of lithography in America is primarily a tale of aspiring artists taking up a new medium as one step in their individual quests for training, recognition, and advancement. These would-be professionals were joined by a host of amateurs, many of them women encouraged by easy access to instruction manuals and materials. The vignette of a young female drawing on stone, featured on the title page of Charles Joseph Hullmandel's *The Art of Drawing on Stone* (London, 1824), demonstrates the determined effort of early lithographic printers to attract an amateur audience. The charitably minded might interpret her as a muse, but the more likely explanation is that her presence conveys the message "it's so simple, even girls can do it."

This feminine representation of the art was subsequently copied on an advertising card for the Boston firm of W. & J. Pendleton, about 1828 (Cat. 7).

American lithography in the early days had no artist superstars to invoke, such as Goya and Delacroix, who in Europe boldly and successfully appropriated the new medium to their own expressive purposes, and created masterpieces treasured far in excess of their significance as early examples of lithographic art. The post-Revolutionary generation of American lithographic practitioners was engaged in quite a different undertaking. Encouraged by a small group of entrepreneurial printer/publishers seeking to capitalize on the increasing demand for images of all sorts, they were helping to shape an American cultural identity. Delacroix's wild animals, and illustrations to *Faust*, and Goya's bullfights, covens of crones, and distressed beauties, while not strictly representational, are definitely representative of Europe in the 1820s. The ferocity, blood, turmoil, and exoticism of these images are resonant of their historical context: the devastation of the Napoleonic wars, the repression of the Bourbon restorations, and the exploitation of Africa and Asia. They are emanations of an old society experiencing the death-throes of absolutism. In contrast, American lithographs of the 1820s reflect a new society brimming with republican idealism.

American lithography emerged and developed during a period of growth and prosperity. Between 1820 and 1830 the population increased by a third. In 1830, 12,866,000 inhabitants lived in twenty-four states, twelve slave and twelve free. The creation of new states had pushed the frontier beyond the Mississippi River. The country was at peace. With the end of the Napoleonic wars in 1815, foreign trade had resumed, and the economy, after the depression of 1819–1822, had revived and would flourish until the next big crash in 1837. The Industrial Revolution was proceeding, and the development of the steamboat, the canal, and the railroad facilitated the movement of goods and people and linked the interior to the commercial centers on the east coast. New York was the largest city and the capital of business. The seat of government was at Washington, then called Washington City. Philadelphia and Boston were the cultural centers. It was primarily in these cities that American lithography came of age.

The first impetus toward lithography in America came from physicians and scientists who wished to have a cheap, easy means of illustrating their writings on natural history.[2] Having heard about lithography, these men attempted to establish local presses, seeking information and supplies from France. In 1807 Dr. Samuel Latham Mitchill (1764–1831) of New York received from de Lasteyrie in Paris a lithographic stone and ink,[3] and the following year the first good American account of the lithographic process was published in the *Medical Repository* for 1808, of which Dr. Mitchill was the co-founder and editor.[4] Thomas Cooper (1759–1840), a physician who was also a retired judge and a professor of Applied Mineralogy and Chemistry at the University of Pennsylvania, talked about lithography in his academic and public lectures. His interest was shared by a circle of physicians and mineralogists living in Philadelphia, most particularly by Dr. Samuel Brown (1769–1830), frequently referred to as Dr. Brown of Alabama, who was soon to become professor of Medicine at Transylvania College in Lexington, Kentucky. A major concern of these men was to find an American substitute for the expensive Bavarian limestone slabs upon which lithographic drawings were traditionally made.[5] Dr. Brown experimented with stone from Pennsylvania and Indiana, and limestone and marble from Kentucky,[6] but none of these possessed the precise degree of hardness and porosity necessary for the correct absorption of water and grease.

In his quest to print images from stone, Dr. Brown enlisted the help of Bass Otis (1784–1861), a successful portrait painter, who is generally credited with making the first American lithograph, although there is debate over which of his prints deserves the title. Some contend that Otis's portrait of the Reverend Abner Kneeland, published as the frontispiece to *A Series of Lectures on the Doctrine of Universal Benevolence* (Philadelphia, 1818) and signed "Bass Otis, Sc.," is an etching on stone and, as such, entitled to the honor of being the first.[7] Supporters of this opinion cite a statement by Senefelder, in the introduction to his treatise of 1818, that "even in Philadelphia . . . lithography is already introduced."[8] Although this remark does not necessarily refer to the Abner Kneeland portrait, it does raise the intriguing possibility that there may have been some communication between Senefelder and Dr. Brown, Judge Cooper, Charles Alexandre Lesueur, or other members of the group. At very least, Senefelder must have read or heard of their efforts.

The print by Otis most frequently acknowledged as the first American lithograph is a small picture of a building by a pond, published in the *Analectic Magazine* for July of 1819, and signed "Bass Otis Lithographic" (Cat. 60). It was printed from a lithographic stone obtained from Munich by Thomas Dobson, a Philadelphia printer and bookseller. Dobson had given the stone to the American Philosophical Society, which in May of 1819 lent it "to Dr. Brown and Mr. Otis for the purpose of making experiments in the art of lithographic engravings."[9] The illustration in the *Analectic* accompanies an article written by Thomas Cooper, who takes pride in pointing out that through the combined efforts of an artist and the learned gentlemen of the American Philosophical Society, one more accomplishment of the old world has been inaugurated into the new:

> In this number we present our readers with a specimen of *American Lithography:* the design and execution from beginning to end — from the drawing to the impression inclusive — is by Mr. B. Otis; who, following the suggestions of judge Cooper, and Dr. Brown, of Alabama, has by means of their hints, and his own more successful improvements, produced the specimen now submitted.[10]

After a few more experiments Otis's involvement with lithography ceased, but notices in the Philadelphia newspapers testify to continued public interest in the subject. The *National Gazette and Literary Register* reported on Neapolitan book printing using various kinds of stone, and also on the patenting of a new lithographic press by J. Ruthven of Edinburgh.[11] A lengthy article under the heading "Selections from Late Scientific Journals — Mr. Hullmandell [*sic*] on Lithography" contained information on preparing and printing lithographic stones. It briefly described the transfer method, engraving on stone, the scraping out of light areas in imitation of wood engraving, and the imitation of aquatint through the use of several stones covered with flat tints. The main point of the article was an endorsement of the chalk (or crayon) method of drawing on stone as the only style that had a "decided superiority," and the chief style practiced in Paris and Munich.[12] Crayon drawing was also the principal style practiced in the United States.

In Philadelphia, at the same time that Bass Otis and Dr. Brown were conducting their experiments, Charles Alexandre Lesueur (1778–1846) was attempting to make lithographs on stones that he had procured from his native France. Lesueur had originally come to America as artist to a geological expedition. He settled in Philadelphia and in 1816 became a member of the Academy of Natural Sciences, publishing many articles that he illustrated himself by means of engraving on copper. Lesueur's lithographic endeavors were hampered by the lack of a professional printer in his adopted city. In 1821 and 1822 he sent his work to New York to be printed by Barnet and Doolittle (Cat. 63), but after that firm folded, he apparently had to do for himself. In 1823 Lesueur wrote to a French zoologist: "If a good lithographer would come to Philadelphia I believe he could prosper by the second year of going into business. Our naturalists feel the need and the importance daily of having such an establishment here, seeing that copper engraving is too expensive and too time consuming. The beautiful impressions which issue from the presses of France are a very strong stimulus for increasing the desire to have something similar."[13]

The New York press to which Lesueur sent his work was established by William Armand Barnet, son of the American consul in Paris, and Isaac Doolittle (both fl. 1816–1822), Barnet's erstwhile collaborator on patenting improvements to steamboats. An article in the *American Journal of Science and the Arts* for October 1821, entitled "Notice of the Lithographic Art," marked their debut, noting that:

> All the drawings in the present number are printed on stone by Messrs. Barnet & Doolittle, whom we are happy to introduce to our readers as artists in this comparatively new department. Having availed themselves in Paris of a regular course of practical instruction, they have brought to this country, not only the skill but the peculiar materials and press necessary to the execution of the art, and are now establishing themselves in New-York . . . Messrs. Barnet & Doolittle have in their possession, a great variety of lithographic prints, which sufficiently evince the adaptedness of the art to an elegant as well as a common style of execution. The finest things done in this way are really very beautiful; and they possess a softness which is peculiarly their own.[14]

Despite this praise, the editor concluded his remarks by saying, "Lithography is not a rival, it is merely an auxiliary to copper plate engraving, which, especially in the higher branches of the art, must still retain that pre-eminence which it possesses."[15] The drawings to which the article refers represent geological strata (Cat. 62) and were drawn on stone by Jacques Gerard Milbert (1766–1840), another French artist/naturalist traveling in the United States. Other work by Barnet & Doolittle is preserved in illustrated books, including a charming Santa Claus story in *The Children's Friend, No. III* (New York, 1821; Cat. 61), for which both the text and illustrations were lithographically printed. The American edition of James Edward Smith's *A Grammar of Botany* (New York, 1822) contains plates drawn on stone by Arthur J. Stansbury (1781–c. 1845), a native of New York, a preacher, and occasional artist. His illustrations were drawn in the pen style and resemble engravings, but a publisher's note proudly proclaims them to be specimens of American lithography.

Despite these successes, letters from Lesueur to William Maclure, the geologist who had initially employed him, indicate that Barnet & Doolittle were having a difficult time. They were able to print only 100 to 150 impressions a day, thus driving their prices up. For 100 copies of the fish drawing they charged Lesueur $2.30, more than double the cost of a copperplate print. In fact, things were so bad Barnet and Doolittle offered to sell their business to Lesueur for $1,000. One of Lesueur's comments is particularly telling. He writes, "Furthermore, in order for lithography to succeed here it is necessary for there to be more connoisseurs of fine arts than there are now. You only find a few individuals who have portfolios full of engravings, and those who have them send them to auction to get rid of them."[16] Given such a discouraging state of affairs, it is not surprising that the firm folded, and by June 1822, Barnet had returned to France.[17] One bright spot in this rather dismal history is the untitled pen lithograph of a woman on a terrace (Cat. 44), drawn on stone by John Rubens Smith (1775–1849) and printed by Barnet & Doolittle. Smith, an English artist and friend of Benjamin West, had probably learned the techniques of lithography before coming to America. His assured, spontaneous handling would be outstanding at any time, but for America in 1821 it was extraordinary.

Washington City was the location of the next lithographic press, which was opened by Henry Stone (fl. 1822–1846) in November of 1822.[18] An article in the *Washington Gazette* for November 15, 1822, hazily described the technique, and stated that Stone was printing from marble, not limestone. The public was invited to visit the shop for instruction and information. To bring in business Stone appealed to the pecuniary interests as well as the vanity of artists, amateurs and inventors, advertising in the *Washington Gazette* for November 20, 1822, that he:

> respectfully informs his friends and the public that having succeeded in establishing a LITHOGRAPHIC PRESS, which is now in daily operation, he tenders his services as LITHOGRAPHER to those who may wish to publish drawings of any description, *Music, Linear Perspective, &c.* — and those who may wish to encourage an infant art, which, from its being in the power of every one who draws, to preserve all their delicacy of style and execution, as well as from its extreme simplicity, economy and expedition, gives a certainty of profit, from such sketches, plans, &c. as would otherwise remain useless in the Port Folios of their ingenious inventors.[19]

Stone did practical, commercial work. His *Plan of the Floor of the House of Representatives,* drawn by Arthur J. Stansbury, was a stock item for every Washington lithographer who succeeded him. He printed patterns for needle work and music scores (sometimes embellished with illustrations); however, his most famous works are the technical illustrations for *The Timber Merchant's Guide,* (Cat. 64) in which he diagrammed methods for cutting up trees to make best use of the lumber for shipbuilding. In this modest, pragmatic fashion, Stone's lithographic press continued in operation until 1826.

As Henry Stone was going out of business, John Blennerhassett Martin (1797–1857) opened a lithographic press in Richmond, Virginia.[20] Irish born, but trained in engraving in New York, Martin moved to Richmond in 1817, working as an engraver and miniature portrait painter prior to becoming a printer of lithographs about 1827. His work is known from a few illustrations for the periodical *Spirit of the Old Dominion* (Cat. 69). The magazine apparently did not have a sufficient audience to survive for more than a year. Likewise, the existence of a commercial lithography firm in a city without a large population was precarious, and few lithographs by Martin were printed there. In 1830, when Martin drew on stone and published a portrait of John Randolph of Roanoke, the work was printed by Cephas G. Childs in Philadelphia. Martin's was the southernmost press in the first decade of American lithography, the principal firms remaining in the north, in New York and Boston.[21]

After the dissolution of the firm of Barnet & Doolittle in New York, Peter Maverick (1780–1831), a native New Yorker, son of an engraver and trained as a engraver himself, incorporated lithography into his commercial repertory in 1824.[22] Treading the same path as his groundbreaking predecessors, Maverick's earliest lithographic efforts were illustrations for articles on natural history that appeared in the *Annals of the Lyceum of Natural History of New York* (1824–1825). The plates were drawn by Maverick himself, his daughters Emily (1803–1850) and Maria (1805–1832), Arthur J. Stansbury, Henry Inman (1801–1846), and others. Single sheet prints by Maverick include portraits, often copied by him from paintings (Cat. 38). Charles Toppan (1796–1874), a banknote engraver who later became president of the American Bank Note Company, drew sentimental subjects for the firm, and James Herring (1794–1867) drew a series of animal prints (Cat. 21 and 22). Maverick was a respected member of the New York art world, and one of the founders of the National Academy of Design in 1826. Until his death in 1831 he continued his work as a general printer, offering copperplate printing, lithography applied to all subjects, and banknote engraving.

Maverick's major lithographic competitor was Anthony Imbert (1794/5–1834), who seems to have established his press in New York in October of 1825.[23] He and Maverick shared the honor of illustrating the

Memoir, published to commemorate the opening of the Erie Canal (Cat. 66), Maverick executing the engravings and Imbert the lithographs. Whereas Maverick looked to England for his models and inspiration, Imbert looked to his native France, where he had served as an officer in the French navy.[24] During his confinement as a British prisoner of war he passed the time improving his skill in drawing and painting. Napoleon was a recurrent subject in his work, and one of his first lithographs in America was indeed a picture of the Emperor's tomb on St. Helena. He later printed *Napoleon au Bivouac* by Gherlando Marsiglia (1792–1850) (Cat. 32). Imbert also lithographed the key (an outline diagram of the figures identified by numbers) to Jacques Louis David's painting of the coronation of Napoleon, *Le Sacre*, exhibited in New York in January 1826. From the outset, lithographs printed by Imbert demonstrated high technical standards and an artistic approach. As a printer he explored a variety of techniques for putting images on stone, including the transfer method (Cat. 2), in which a drawing made on specially treated paper is laid face down on a stone and run through the press to transfer the image, which is then printed in the usual manner. This method had the advantage of portability, and eliminated the necessity of draw ing or writing in reverse.

Himself a painter, Imbert associated with other French artists, including Edme Rousseau (fl. 1825–1843), who ran an "Academy of Drawing and Painting in Miniature," and managed the tour of David's *Le Sacre*. Imbert and Rousseau collaborated on an instruction book entitled *Lithographic Principles of Landscape Drawing* (ca. 1826–27), sold by subscription and issued in parts. Other early collaborators included the architect Alexander Jackson Davis (1803–1892), who made his first drawing on stone — a copy of his own painting of Castle Garden, a New York amusement center — on November 24, 1825, just as Imbert was getting started. Again in 1827 Davis drew on stone for Imbert eight architectural views for a projected series of *Views of Public Buildings, Edifices and Monuments, in the Principal Cities of the United States*.[25]

Imbert's press gained welcome publicity and prestige when he was selected to print the lithographic illustrations for the *Memoir* issued to celebrate the opening of the Erie Canal (New York, 1825; Cat. 66). More than thirty-five lithographs were drawn on stone by Imbert and a number of other artists, including George Catlin (1796–1872), later famous for his depictions of Native Americans. Association with an event of such civic importance brought Imbert welcome publicity and connected him with people of power and influence. Artists who were members of the venerable American Academy of the Fine Arts and the upstart National Academy of Design drew on stone and also took their work to Imbert, and his productions included important landscapes such as Thomas Cole's (1801–1848) *Distant View of the Slides That Destroyed the Whilley Family* (Cat. 11), and Marsiglia's uncommonly beautiful views of Catskill Falls and Niagara Falls. Just six years earlier, Barnet & Doolittle had languished for lack of such recognition and interest; now American culture was coming of age and Imbert was learning how to cultivate the artistic community.

However, subscriptions to the drawing book were slow in coming, and only eight plates of the ambitious *Views of Public Edifices* series were issued, despite their high quality and modest price of fifty cents each.[26] The problem was that of audience sophistication, or lack of it, and no substantial market developed for his work. Imbert had started his business by offering interesting framing prints of good quality, but by 1830 he turned to printing and publishing cheap work: sheet music and covers, small prints for scrapbooks and craft work, and caricatures. There was a great popular market for caricatures, and Imbert used the capacity of lithography to produce cheap copies quickly to satisfy the demand.

Some of Imbert's difficulties probably arose from increased competition. Unlike Maverick, he did not have an engraving department to fall back on, and several other New York firms had begun to offer lithographic services. Prosper Desobry (fl. 1824–1844) had worked as a letterer for Imbert in 1827,[27] and at some point, possibly as early as 1824, he was in lithographic partnership with another unknown called Chanou. A frontispiece for bound sheet music (Cat. 53) issued from Number 56 Exchange Place documents this collaboration. In 1828 Desobry had his own lithographic business and continued in New York until 1842, printing wall and album pictures, sheet music covers, and book illustrations.[28] Imbert's competition also included Anthony Fleetwood (ca. 1800–1860), a lithographer from Liverpool, England, who was operating a "Lithographic Printing Office" in New York by the fall of 1826.[29] One suspects that at this date he was primarily a job printer, not challenging Imbert's position as a printer of artistic lithographs, but their competition for the bread-and-butter work would have been fierce, particularly when both shops were located on Murray Street.[30]

In the autumn of 1825, at the same time Imbert was setting up shop in New York, the brothers John Pendleton (1798–1866) and William S. Pendleton (1795–1879) established the first lithographic enterprise in Boston.[31] William, and perhaps John, had been trained as a copperplate engraver, but both seem to have been primarily impresarios and entrepreneurs. They sought to launch their lithographic business by agreeing to produce for publication lithographs copied from Gilbert Stuart's (1755–1828) oil portraits of the first five presidents[32] (Cat. 33–37). The venture was to be supported by John Doggett (1780–1857), proprietor of a looking glass and carpet store that also contained an art gallery called Doggett's Repository, in which Doggett had exhibited, between January and March of 1822, the Stuart paintings that were to be copied.

The vicissitudes of this project demonstrate the rocky state of lithography in America and its dependence on French expertise. William Pendleton, who was working as an engraver in partnership with Abel Bowen (1790–1850), one of Boston's most prominent engravers and publishers, purchased a lithographic press and stones that had been imported by a Boston merchant named Thaxter.[33] Meanwhile, John Pendleton was in France as a purchasing agent for John Doggett. His traveling companion was the American painter Alvan Fisher (1792–1863), who spent some of his time assembling an assortment of engravings, lithographs, illustrated books and albums which were to be auctioned in Boston.[34] Together they were given a demonstration of the lithographic process, possibly by Milbert, the French artist who had been working in New York in 1821 and whose drawings were printed by Barnet & Doolittle.[35] In October or early November 1825, John Pendleton returned to Boston, bringing lithographic stones bearing copies of the Stuart presidential portraits — drawn by a French artist of the first rank — a press, and also a French pressman to run off the impressions.[36] According to Doggett's son-in-law, who was in charge of gathering subscriptions for the series, John Pendleton's first attempt to print these stones, in January 1826, was a fiasco. Apparently fewer than one hundred satisfactory impressions were pulled. If indeed a French pressman was present, he was no more a master of printing than John Pendleton, who finally announced that he — Pendleton — must go to France, or send someone there to have the work completed. Doggett repudiated the contract, with considerable bad feeling generated by the loss of money and reputation.

Two years later, the joint venture was resumed. John Pendleton returned to France, again on business for Doggett. It is not known what material he brought back this time, but after his return to Boston Doggett was able to fill orders for large numbers of presidential sets, shipping them "nicely framed & packed" to ports as distant as New Orleans.[37] Pendleton is not mentioned in the prospectus or credited on the prints, but references in the letter books of John Doggett & Co. imply that he was in charge of the American printing.[38] By this time his litho-

graphic press would have been operating for two years, and prints pulled from it had won two silver medals, the highest honor, from the Franklin Institute in Philadelphia as the best specimens of lithography to be executed in the United States (Cat. 41 and 43). Doggett christened his series *The American Kings*. They are beautifully drawn and printed, and set the standard for lithographic portraiture in America.

The making of *The American Kings* proceeded simultaneously with the establishment of the lithographic business of the brothers Pendleton. They recruited local painters — Francis Alexander (1800–1880), Thomas Edwards (1795–1869), David Claypoole Johnston (1798–1865), and John Ritto Penniman (1783–1830) — to make lithographs using materials supplied by John Pendleton. Examples by Edwards and Johnston, and an unsigned design of a vase of flowers presumed to be by John Pendleton himself (Cat. 65), were published in the *Boston Monthly Magazine* for December 1825, to accompany an article on lithography. The accompanying article quotes extensively from Senefelder's account of his discovery, indicating that in addition to having proper stones and drawing materials, the Boston artists were well supplied with technical manuals such as the English translation of *A Complete Course of Lithography* (London, 1819). Another lengthy quotation "from Raucourt's work on Lithography" suggests that a copy of Charles Joseph Hullmandel's English translation of Antoine Raucourt de Charville's *Manual of Lithography* (London, 1821) was on hand. The lithograph of a mill and waterwheel furnished by D. C. Johnston as an illustration to accompany the article is a sketchy copy, in reverse, of Plate 15 in Hullmandel's own manual, *The Art of Drawing on Stone* (London, 1824). In addition, it is known that Abel Bowen, who instructed and encouraged many of the figures associated with Boston lithography, owned a copy of Godefroy Engelmann's *Manuel du dessinateur lithographe* (Paris, 1822).[39]

The partnership of Pendleton & Bowen dissolved early in 1826, and in February William Pendleton announced the formation of his own engraving business in partnership with John, "who will add to the Establishment the advantage of Lithographic Printing,"[40] The arrival in Boston of Rembrandt Peale (1778–1860), who took a studio adjacent to the Pendleton shop and used its facilities to make lithographs, helped to boost the firm's reputation. The painter's reputation was well known, and his large composition *The Court of Death* had been on an exhibition tour managed by the Pendletons.[41] Peale was the most mature and accomplished American-born artist to take up the lithographic crayon. He produced some fine original compositions on stone, most notably a view of

Jefferson's Rock, drawn from nature near Harper's Ferry and printed in Boston ca. 1827. His *Patriae Pater* (Cat. 41), copied on stone from a portrait of Washington painted for the United States Senate, ranks as one of the great American portrait lithographs. However, Peale's *Lithographic Sketches, Memoranda of Form and Character* (Cat. 42 and 67) is a far cry from the tour de force artist portfolios published in Europe. Intended as an advertisement for the Pendleton firm, this modest pamphlet contains eight derivative plates demonstrating virtuosity in subject matter, but not in handling — all are rendered in the same crayon style. Printed with letterpress commentary, it more closely relates to the entertaining collections and comic annuals issued by many artists to supplement their more serious work.

In addition to painters, the Boston engravers Joseph Andrews (1806–1873), John Cheney (1801–1885) and Seth Wells Cheney (1810–1856), James Eddy (1806–1888), and William Hoogland (ca. 1795–1832), were persuaded to draw on stone. A. J. Davis, who had drawn buildings for Imbert in 1825, made two trips to Boston during the winters of 1827 and 1828 to study the architectural books in Boston Athenæum. While in Boston he drew buildings to be printed and sold by the Pendletons, including the Massachusetts State House (Cat. 14), considered by Davis and others to be the finest example of architectural drafting in lithography produced in the United States to that time. Davis also drew the hotels and commercial buildings surrounding the Pendleton shop.

Lithographic shops also afforded young artists the opportunity to get practical training as apprentice copyists and draftsmen. Prior to 1830, the Pendletons employed M. E. D. Brown (1810–1896) and Benjamin Nutting (1803?–1887) in this capacity. The redoubtable Moses Swett, (1804–1838), previously an ornamental painter, made his first attempt on stone in January 1826, a small picturesque vignette of a castle surrounded by trees, probably printed at the Pendleton shop.[42] From then on, Swett produced a steady stream of drawings for the Pendletons. He emerges as an unsung hero of early American lithography, prolific and skilled in rendering a variety of subjects. Capable of designing his own compositions, he invariably signed his original work "M. Swett inv. and del.", meaning inventor (of the design) and delineator (Cat. 45–49).

The year 1828 saw a marked increase in lithographic activity in the United States, with the establishment of competing firms in Philadelphia, New York, and Boston. In Philadelphia there had been no significant lithographic activity since the experiments of Bass Otis and Lesueur, but in the spring or summer of 1828, William B. Lucas (d. 1833), a gilder and proprietor of a looking-glass store,

took an interest.[43] One of the earliest lithographs printed by Lucas was a theatrical portrait, *Cowell as Crack in the Turnpike Gate*, drawn on stone by Hugh Bridport (1794–c. 1868), a miniature painter. It probably dates from June 1828, and bears the imprint "Lucas's Lithography." Lucas took as a partner David Kennedy, also a gilder.[44] It is possible that Edmund Brewster (fl. 1818–1839), a Philadelphia portrait painter, took advantage of their services, since in April and May of 1829 he advertised a lithographed portrait by his own hand and also a weekly scrapbook of lithographic illustrations. W. L. Breton (fl. 1830–1839), a painter of ships and views, drew churches for Kennedy & Lucas, as well as historical illustrations printed by them for John F. Watson's *Annals of Philadelphia* (1830). Lucas himself drew *The Orphan* (Cat. 31) and other prints. He died in 1833, and soon after his three presses, 8,000 pounds of lithographic stone, and other materials were disposed of at an executor's sale. Judging from what has survived, the firm's output of images appears to have been small, their work mainly consisting of ephemera, job printing, and music, of which *The Chaplet* (Cat. 52) is a charming example.

Certainly the lithographs of Kennedy & Lucas were overshadowed by those produced under the direction of Cephas G. Childs (1793–1871), an established engraver.[45] It is said that Childs persuaded John Pendleton to come from Boston to Philadelphia to join him in the business that opened in the summer of 1829 under the name Pendleton, Kearny & Childs. Francis Kearny (1785–1837), the other principal, was an engraver, and the firm offered both copperplate and lithographic printing. Childs' promotion of the artistic side of the business was commented upon in the *United States Gazette* for September 9, 1828:

> It is the intention of Mr. Childs, and the gentlemen connected with him, to present to the public specimens of lithographic drawing that shall tend to beget a taste for the arts, and introduce some of its pleasing products at a price within the command of almost every person. It is a proof of Mr. Childs' love of the arts and of his intentions to make improvements in his own establishment, that he exhibits to visitors specimens of Parisian lithographs superior to those of his own drawing, but which will scarcely claim superiority a year hence, if the improvements of the last month may be considered as a criterion for future advancement.[46]

Artists drawing on stone for Pendleton, Kearny & Childs included Kearny himself, Moses Swett, the experienced lithographic draftsman from Boston, and Hugh Bridport, the miniature painter who also drew for Lucas. Most notably, they employed Albert Newsam (1809–1864),

a deaf mute who had been educated at the famous
Pennsylvania Institution for the Deaf and Dumb, where
he was given drawing lessons by George Catlin and Hugh
Bridport. In 1827, Newsam was placed with Childs, who
taught him to engrave on steel before moving on to lithography in 1829.[47] That year Newsam was entrusted with
a major commission, to copy on stone a portrait of Henry
Clay after a painting by Joseph Wood (1778–1830). His
success foreshadowed his future as the principal lithographic portrait draftsman in Philadelphia and one of
the best in the country up to the Civil War.

The partnership of Pendleton, Kearny & Childs lasted
long enough to get the business going and then dissolved.
John Pendleton settled in New York, where he ran a shop
offering lithography, engraving and printing, and also
imported prints and artist supplies.[48] By January 1, 1830,
Childs was in sole command of the Philadelphia firm. In
December of that year, in order to strengthen the firm's
position, he took Henry Inman (1801–1846) of New York
as a partner, who, in addition to painting oil portraits to
be copied, learned to draw them directly on the stone.
Other artists associated with the firm included Thomas
Doughty (1793–1856), landscape painter, who for a time
had a studio at Childs' business address at 80 Walnut
Street; George Lehman (d. 1870), another landscape
painter, who drew views for the firm and later became a
partner; and E. W. Clay (1799–1857), who drew spirited
caricatures.

The wheel horse of this team, however, was Albert
Newsam. Talented and reliable, Newsam churned out the
portraits that were the mainstay of the shop. One of Child's
advertising gambits solicited families to bring in oil portraits to be copied on stone by Newsam, at a charge of
$25.00 for twenty-five copies. The stone was retained
against future need, much as portrait photographers were
to operate later in the century.[49] Childs was successful in
integrating himself into the artistic community, and favorable editorial notices in the Philadelphia papers kept his
lithographs before the public. Traveling to Paris in 1831
to visit the lithographic shops, he returned with P. S. Duval
(fl. 1831–1879), an experienced pressman who was an
important addition to the firm. Despite his good instincts,
Childs derived no steady profit from lithography. When he
finally left the business in 1834 he owed money to Newsam
and to Duval, who succeeded him as a proprietor of the
firm. By keeping pace with technological innovations
such as steam powered printing presses and full color
printing — called chromolithography — Duval was eventually able to turn lithography into a profitable enterprise.

John Pendleton's departure from Boston in 1828 may
have influenced the formation of the second lithographic

press in that city.[50] A splinter group comprised of Moses
Swett, Thomas Edwards, and Benjamin Nutting broke
away from the Pendleton shop in Graphic Court and
formed their own lithographic establishment in
September 1828, christening it the Senefelder Lithographic Company.[51] Initially, Swett served as superintendent of the firm, and Edwards, who was also active as a
miniature painter and drawing master, was the principal
portraitist. They were joined and supported by William
B. Annin (fl. 1813–1839), George Girdler Smith (1795–
1878), and James Kidder (1793–1837), all of whom had
been associated with Abel Bowen. Annin and Smith were
engravers who apparently oversaw the business aspect of
the firm, and Kidder, who was an artist, aquatinter and
engraver, became the firm's principal landscape artist,
producing serene views rendered in subtle tonalities (Cat.
28–30). The range of printing offered by the Senefelder
Company is graphically displayed in an ambitious trade
card designed and drawn by Moses Swett. (Cat. 49).

Works from this press received frequent favorable
notices in *The Bower of Taste*, a Boston magazine edited
by Katharine A. Ware (1797–1843), who was described as
"a poetess of no ordinary ability."[52] Her magazine sponsored a literary contest for a "Prize Tale," to be published
with an illustration devised from one of its most prominent scenes. The award for 1828 went to "The Pirates, or
Errors of Public Justice," which was published with a
lithograph by Thomas Edwards.[53] Edwards received frequent commendations for his lithographic portraits of
eminent characters, and for an admirably clear drawing
book.[54] *The Bower of Taste* also praised the lithographic
work of Margaret Clark Snow (fl. 1827–1831), who gave
lessons in perspective, drawing and painting at her home
on Franklin Street, and contributed illustrations to the
magazine.[55] Mrs. Snow's lithographs were printed by
both the Senefelder and the Pendleton presses. In 1831
she married William S. Pendleton.

Despite a large and impressive output, the Senefelder
Lithographic Company did not survive. A removal notice
in the *Boston Daily Advertiser* for December 13, 1830,
states that the press had moved to Nos. 59 and 61
Cornhill, and that Edwards, Kidder, Nutting, and the
engraving firm of Annin & Smith had taken studios in
the same building. Shortly after this move, the Senefelder
Company was bought out by William S. Pendleton,
although Annin, Smith, Edwards, and Nutting continued
to issue lithographs under the imprint Annin, Smith &
Co.'s Lithography until 1833.[56]

At the same time the Pendleton and Senefelder presses
were competing in Boston, an extraordinary man named
Joseph Dixon (1799–1869) became interested in lithogra-

phy. Dixon was a precocious inventor, and had mastered letterpress printing and wood engraving before experimenting with lithographic printing in 1828 and 1829. He made trial proofs at both the Pendleton and Senefelder presses, dating and annotating impressions drawn by T. West (fl. 1828–1829) and by J. Webb (fl. 1823–1829), the latter a Salem, Massachusetts, artist who also drew the lithographs printed on Dixon's own Franklin Press in Salem (Cat. 50 and 51).[57] In his fascination with the technological aspects of lithography, Dixon harks back to the physicians who had instigated the first lithographic attempts in the United States a decade earlier.

Moses Swett left Boston for Baltimore in 1830 and there formed the partnership of Endicott & Swett, the last major firm of the decade. Swett's partner was George Endicott (1802–1848), an ornamental painter. In their quarters at Graphic Hall they offered engraving as well as lithography, and sold their own prints and those made by others in their "picture room."[58] Endicott also continued to accept painting commissions. By December of 1831, however, the partners had moved on to New York, where George Endicott went on to manage G. & W. Endicott, in partnership with his younger brother William. The firm's successor, Endicott & Co. (1852–1886), was one of the great American lithographic establishments. Moses Swett died in 1838, when he was thirty-four, unfortunately without writing the history of American lithography that he had promised William Dunlap, an early American art historian.

Early American lithographic firms shared some common characteristics, the most notable of which was that most proprietors were engravers first, and continued to offer engraving as part of their printing services. Anthony Imbert seems to have been unique among the major early lithographers in that he devoted himself exclusively to lithography; his promotion of the transfer method, for artistic as well as practical purposes, was also unusual. The early lithographic firms, and indeed their successors into the twentieth century, did all types of job printing — cards, tickets, labels, forms, facsimiles, maps and plans — and this work gave them common ties to the general business community.

These firms also pursued the artistic community with fervor, in order to gain prestige, publicity, and an expanded market. Imbert, the Pendleton brothers, and Childs particularly pursued this avenue. In many cases, artists occupied studio space in the same building as the presses, or in adjacent space. Thomas Doughty's connection with Childs has been cited. Pendleton's Lithography shared the Graphic Court address with Rembrandt Peale and George

Harvey (ca. 1800/01–1878), a landscape and miniature painter.[59] The Senefelder Lithographic Company may be viewed as an artists' collaborative, its address shifting with the studios of its members. The participation of painters naturally widened the venues in which lithography could be seen.[60]

The cultivation of amateurs was important to lithographic businesses in their formative years. Most shops provided free instruction, and could furnish stones and drawing materials. It is possible that American lithographic printers followed the practice common in Europe at this time of leasing stones to amateurs and artists with a contract to print a certain number of copies.[61] A letter written by Louisa Davis Minot (1788–1858) on April 8, 1826, soon after completing her first attempt at lithographic drawing, *View on the Kennebeck* (Cat. 39), gives many details of the experience. Writing from Boston to a friend in Gardiner, Maine, Mrs. Minot says: "It is very easy to learn to draw on the stone, but it takes more time and requires more nicety than drawing in pencil. If Emma [apparently the recipient's daughter] should be inclined to try it, there will be no difficulty in transporting the stones from this place to Gardiner and back again to be struck off. You know, I presume that we have a Lithographic press in Boston. Miss Scollay has done some views of Trenton falls, very beautifully, in this style."[62] Both Louisa Minot's work and that of Catherine Scollay (1783–1863; Cat. 43) were printed at the Pendleton press.

Amateur work was privately distributed to families and friends, often being preserved in albums or scrapbooks. The album of Mary Jane Derby (1807–1892), daughter of a Salem, Massachusetts, merchant, contains, in addition to her own lithographs (Cat. 15–16) and drawings, lithographs by James F. Colman (fl. 1828–1831; Cat. 12), the son of a local minister.[63] Colman's lithographs were also included in scrapbooks assembled by Eliza Susan Quincy (1798–1884), eldest daughter of Josiah Quincy (1772–1864), Mayor of Boston and President of Harvard, whose collection is a lively mix of newspaper clippings, prints of all kinds, and pencil, wash, and watercolor drawings by Miss Quincy and her friends.[64] Most importantly, one volume contains early American lithographs, including Eliza Susan Quincy's first effort on stone, dated 1826.[65] Several other lithographs bearing Pendleton and Senefelder imprints are signed with only the initials of the delineators. Beneath these Miss Quincy has written their full names, thus identifying two other amateurs who took up the lithographic crayon, "J. F. C.," or James F. Colman, and "S. C. C.," or Susan Cabot.[66]

The Derby album and the Quincy scrapbook reveal the role of drawing in the lives of affluent Americans. It was an entertainment, a medium of social exchange, a form of memorializing, an *aide memoir*. It was also a practical skill, necessary to professions such as architecture and engineering. Drawing instructors were among the first to take up lithography, and it became a favored medium for drawing books, of which John Rubens Smith's *Compendium of Picturesque Anatomy* (Cat. 68) is an outstanding example. The role of lithography in fostering this aspect of American cultural development is expressed in an editor's note published in the *Boston Daily Advertiser* for March 24, 1825:

DRAWING

This elegant accomplishment, which is esteemed so necessary a part of polite education in Europe, is constantly becoming more popular in this country. The best instructors are liberally encouraged, and the attention of young persons is early directed to the happiest efforts of genius and skill, while no pains are spared by judicious parents to improve their taste and guide their exertions. In this state of things, it is gratifying to observe the means of improvement, which are afforded by the importation of prints, furnishing admirable exercises for the young pupil, in every step of his progress, from the simplest delineation of rural scenery and figures, to the fine characteristic touches of Wilkie and Westall. Lithographic prints in particular, from their close resemblance to delicate penciling, are very well adapted for early exercises.[67]

The passage quoted above alludes to a cultural climate that was becoming increasingly more favorable to lithography. Americans were developing a taste for prints, as evidenced by a noticeable increase in newspaper advertisements for sales of prints between 1820 and 1825. By 1830 such advertisements were common and the descriptions of the merchandise became more specific. Engravings formed the bulk of the offerings, but around 1825 lithographs began to be mentioned as well. Almost invariably the prints were described as originating from Paris. They came from Europe by ship and were usually sold at auction, in lots, direct from the importer.[68] Increased importation of European prints helped American lithographers by developing public taste and graphic awareness, and providing models for artists to copy. However, they also injured American lithographers by retaining the high end market share, since European prints were perceived as better, and worth a higher price.

Seeking a share of the burgeoning print market, American lithographers published selected images as commercial ventures, making display and sales areas part of their printing premises. In addition to selling the products of their own presses, lithographers such as the Pendletons also sold American prints made in other cities, a variety of imported prints, and sheet music with lyrics in English, French, and Italian.[69] Lithographic prints were also sold by booksellers, stationers, and fancy goods merchants, and even circulating libraries.[70] William Simpson, who sold reticules, stationary, games, books, and imported prints at his shop on Chestnut Street in Philadelphia, made a patriotic pitch for the American lithographs on offer there: "Ladies and gentlemen, lovers of the Fine Arts, desirous of encouraging native merit, are respectfully invited to call at the store of the subscriber, and inspect a beautiful collection of *Lithographic Prints,* when they will have an opportunity of judging to what a degree of perfection the art of Lithography has arrived in this country."[71] Sheet music publishers, particularly George Melksham Bourne in New York and R. H. Hobson in Philadelphia, sold American and European prints, picture albums, illustrated books, etc. in their shops.[72]

The relationship between lithography and music publishing dates back to the earliest years of Senefelder's discovery. In the United States, however, the use of lithography for printing music never caught on, even though it was less expensive. It was felt that lithographed music lacked the incisive finish of engraved notes, and it was considered cut rate.

Music publishers did, however, avail themselves of lithography's capacity to cheaply provide decorative effects that would attract the eye and engage the sentiments of a largely amateur audience. Publishers made use of lithographed illustrations on decorative title pages intended for bound volumes of sheet music (Cat. 53), and illustrated headings on first sheets, some of the earliest of these being produced by Henry Stone in Washington City. The first use of a lithographic illustration on a separately printed cover sheet occurred in 1826, with the publication of *The Log House* (Cat. 56). A variety of lithographic techniques lent themselves to the demands of sheet music title pages, on which elaborate lettering in many different styles could be combined with eye-catching illustrations usually drawn in the crayon manner.

One of the most important music publishers of the decade was George M. Bourne, of New York. Sheet music issuing from his Depository of Arts on Broadway was considered the height of elegance, praised for the quality of the music engraving, much of it by T. Birch, and for the illustrations, which were often printed on colored paper (Cat. 57 and 58).[73] *The Log House* was followed by an ever increasing spate of sentimental, romantic, comic, and topical covers, to the point where sheet music illustration became an economic mainstay of American lithographic shops.

The style and content of early American lithographs generally followed European models. Many first attempts on stone were copied from picturesque landscapes featuring castles, ruins, and rustic buildings, and commercially published lithographs were often copied from works by French, English, and Italian artists. A look at the prints that make up the tongue-in-cheek figure of *The Connoisseur* (Cat. 77) gives a sense of the popular taste of the time. Subjects include portraits of Washington, Lafayette, Napoleon, Byron, and Shakespeare, as well as landscapes, seascapes, and cityscapes. Animals abound. In addition to *The Puppies* (Cat. 22) and *The Kittens* (Cat. 21), there is a fox, a peacock, and some poor creature that has been hung up to cure. A few flower prints, forming the collar, shoes, and socks, complete the aesthetic attire of *The Connoisseur*.

The European taste for picturesque scenery was readily adopted by American artists. Some of the landscapes in this exhibition are souvenirs of personal travel (Cat. 39 and 70); others are commercially inspired depictions of popular tourist attractions (Cat. 2, 10, and 43). The presence of Thomas Cole in the roster of artists (Cat. 11) reminds us that in this decade the Hudson River school of painters was capitalizing on America's greatest free natural resource, her landscape scenery.

Romanticism, with its emphasis on individual liberty, also had great appeal for Americans. Its icons were the figures of Byron (Cat. 40) and Napoleon (Cat. 32), both heroes in the romantic mode, men who forged their own destinies and lived with grand gestures. Romanticism also suited the inclination of Americans to explore and exploit their vast, wild continent. The excesses associated with Romanticism, however, probably prevented its taking too strong a hold in a country shaped by strict religious principles and hard practical necessities. Americans were much more inclined toward the virtue and legitimacy implicit in the Classical mode.

Since the Renaissance, a taste for the antique has been a sign of high culture. That Americans subscribed to this notion is demonstrated in many ways, including the foundation of numerous lyceums and athenaeums. In 1825 a weekly magazine to be named *Parthenon* was proposed, to be "printed from stone by a process which is designated by the term Typolithy and which unites by one preparation of the press Pictorial Illustration with the printed text."[74] The journal would be devoted to "music, the arts of design and polite literature."[75] Fashionable gift books, tokens of affection and esteem, frequently adopted classical motifs. The title page to the *Cabinet* (Cat. 8) shows Athena, goddess of wisdom, presiding over female personifications of art and literature, whose presence, and the rays of light emanating from the title, guarantee that the contents will be inspired and illuminating.

The gods of Greece were also evoked in the naive, but earnest frontispiece to *Gunn's Domestic Medicine* (Cat. 74), published in Tennessee in 1830, which shows Apollo presenting Asclepius to the centaur Chiron to be instructed in the arts of healing. For such an image to adorn a home health manual devoted to medicinal plants found in the southern and western United States is startling. In this context the classical imagery has little to do with elite culture, however, but rather evokes the purity and wisdom of ancient Greece, the cradle of democracy.

Many prints in the present exhibition demonstrate how deeply the classical ideal pervaded the built environment. Before the Revolution and for a period after it, American architecture, particularly in conservative Boston, followed the English neoclassical style. In the domestic sphere, this style is exemplified by Samuel McIntire's (1757–1811) alterations to the Derby House, in Salem, Massachusetts (Cat. 15), which had corner pilasters, a pedimented entryway, urns on the fence posts, and swags on the carriage house facade. The work of Charles Bulfinch (1763–1844) also adapted English style. His design for the Massachusetts State House (1795–1798), as represented in the Pendleton lithograph from measured drawings by A. J. Davis (Cat. 14), combined Greek pediment, Corinthian colonnade, and Roman dome with Palladian windows.

Beginning in 1820, a new architectural interpretation of the antique, called Greek Revival, shaped most of the public buildings and many private structures erected during the expansive decade before 1830. The bolder, more rugged forms of the Greek Revival style can be seen in Alexander Parris's (1780–1852) Quincy Market complex (Cat. 13), completed in 1826. The columns of the central Quincy Market building are Doric. The Ionic mode is represented by the columns of the Providence Arcade (Cat. 45), a shopping mall, then as now. Triangular pediments and columns also adorned the facades of schools, which often perched on hills like Acropolises of learning (Cat. 19). In H. Corbin Kidder's (1801–1874) view of Amherst College (Cat. 3), the looming forest and humble cabin in close proximity to the fine new school buildings are visual manifestations of the transformation taking place throughout America as the subsistence mentality of the frontier evolved into the desire for civilized amenities such as grand structures and higher education.

The classical temple motif also abounds in generic buildings featured in a wide variety of prints of the period. A drawing book pastiche titled *Temple of Jupiter* was the subject of Mary Jane Derby's first drawing on stone (Cat. 16). In the sheet music illustration for *Isle of Beauty Fare Thee Well!* (Cat. 57), rays of sunlight highlight the columns of a shrine perched high on an enchanted isle. The urn, an important ornament in the classical vocabulary, also makes frequent appearances. It forms part of the setting for the vibrant beauty portrayed by John Rubens Smith (Cat. 44). In the "mourning print" lithographed by M. E. D. Brown (Cat. 5), an urn sits atop the gravestone, and beside it stands a grieving woman dressed *à la grecque*, wearing a short-sleeved chiton with a chalmis draped over her arms. This frequently repeated design was the most respectful and elegantly correct tribute that could be rendered to a departed family member.

Nowhere is the classical identification of America's political and cultural idealism more clearly manifested than in Rembrandt Peale's portrait of Washington as *Patriae Pater* (Cat. 41). The father of his country, in civilian dress, is viewed through a circular opening of carved stone, bordered by the leaves and fruit of the oak, the tree of Zeus. The head of the god himself is carved on the keystone. Washington as Zeus, Athena as guardian of culture, Chiron as medical advisor, and justice, bounty, and knowledge issuing from colonnaded porticoes: in this imagery the expectation of a new golden age is palpable.

In this lively period of prosperity and expansion the lithographic printing shop was a cultural nexus, frequented by a diverse section of the populace because of the variety of goods and services offered there. Businessmen placed orders for the job printing that facilitated commerce, government officials ordered maps, promoters ordered advertisements, and cultural and benevolent societies ordered certificates. Authors went seeking illustrations for the scientific publications so necessary "to advance the high destinies of our Republic."[76] The shop was a meeting place for amateur and professional artists, a place of art instruction, and a resort for persons pursuing the cultivated leisure activities of music and picture collecting.

In this stimulating atmosphere, tinged with the flush of the new, American lithography came of age. The very uncertainty of the enterprise created a special climate that unfortunately was lost after 1830. As the art became established, inventors and experimenters went on to new pursuits. Amateurs and painters largely forsook the scene, and fewer women drew on stone as compared to the first decade. After 1830 lithographic firms proliferated in the major cities, and became more financially stable and longer lived, and with commercial success there came a greater degree of predictability. Treatments became formulaic and shops developed recognizable styles. Lithographic draftsmen became well trained professionals, often pursuing life-long careers. Not until the artistic revival of the twentieth century did American lithography regain the freshness, variety, and vitality that had accrued to it in its cradle stage.

NOTES

1. Senefelder described his discovery and development of lithography in *Vollstandiges Lehrbuch der Steindruckery* (Munich and Vienna, 1818). For a modern English reprint see Alois Senefelder, *A Complete Course of Lithography* (London, 1919; New York: Da Capo Press, 1968).

2. Philip J. Weimerskirch, "Naturalists and the Beginnings of Lithography in America," in *From Linnaeus to Darwin: Commentaries on the History of Biology and Geology* (London: Society for the History of Natural Science, 1985), 167–177; and "Lithographic Stone in America," *Printing History*, 11, no. 1 (1989), 2–15.

3. Charles Philibert de Lasteyrie, Comte de Saillant, was the son-in-law of the Marquis de Lafayette. He set up the first commercially successful lithographic shop in Paris in 1816.

4. The account consisted of letters to Dr. Mitchill from de Lasteyrie and from David Bailie Warden, on the staff of the American consulate in Paris. The *Medical Repository* account was summarized in the *National Intelligencer* (Washington, DC) for January 8, 1808. See Weimerskirch, "Lithographic Stone in America," 2–3.

5. Motivated by similar concerns, exploration for native lithographic stone was also being conducted in England, France, Italy, and Switzerland. See Michael Twyman, "Lithographic Stone and the Printing Trade in the Nineteenth Century," *Journal of the Printing Historical Society*, 8 (1972), 1–41.

6. Weimerskirch, "Lithographic Stone in America," 3, 5. The quest for lithographic stone is also described in [Thomas Cooper], "Lithography," *Analectic Magazine*, 14 (July 1819), 67–73.

7. Joseph Jackson, "Bass Otis, America's First Lithographer," *Pennsylvania Magazine of History and Biography*, 37 (1913), 385–94. Michael Twyman and Philip J. Weimerskirch are currently working on a definitive resolution of this controversy.

8. Senefelder (Da Capo reprint), 85.

9. Record of the Secretary of the American Philosophical Society, quoted in Jackson, 388.

10. Cooper, 67. Some believe that this print is also an etching on stone, as were Senefelder's first prints from stone, and not a true lithograph made by the chemical printing process. Richard Wolfe has pointed out that in this respect American lithography followed the course of Senefelder's own invention process. It is Wolfe's opinion that Dr. Jacob Bigelow used etched stones to print the colored illustrations for his *American Medical Botany* (Boston, 1817–1820). The printers of Bigelow's illustrations were Annin & Smith, copperplate engravers who later became superintendents of the Senefelder Lithographic Company, established in Boston in 1828. See Richard J. Wolfe, *Jacob Bigelow's "American Medical Botany,"* (North Hills, PA.: Bird and Bull Press, 1979).

11. October, 18, 1820, p. 3; November, 22, 1820, p. 3.

12. *National Gazette and Literary Register*, December 27, 1820, p. 4.

13. Letter quoted in Ann Shelby Blum, *Picturing Nature. American Nineteenth-Century Zoological Illustration* (Princeton: Princeton University Press, 1993), 52.

14. [Benjamin Silliman], *American Journal of Science and the Arts*, 4 (1822), 170.

15. Ibid.

16. Lesueur's letters to Maclure, in the Workingmen's Institute Library, New Harmony, Indiana, are quoted in Weimerskirch, "Naturalists and the Beginnings of Lithography in America," 171. Lesueur's letter is dated March 29, 1821.

17. Weimerskirch, "Lithographic Stone in America," 6.

18. Henry Stone was born in England, son of Charles Henry Stone, Royal Navy, who came to the United States with his sons Henry (the lithographer) and James, and settled in Elizabethtown, NJ, working as a miller. Information on Stone is derived from Edith A. Wright and Josephine A. McDevitt, "Henry Stone, Lithographer," *Antiques*, 34 (July 1938). 16–19.

19. Quoted in Wright and McDevitt, 16.

20. Information about Martin is derived from Harry T. Peters, *America on Stone* (Garden City, NY: Doubleday, Doran and Company, 1931), 273; and from Charles Henry Taylor, "Some Notes on Early American Lithography," *Proceedings of the American Antiquarian Society*, n.s. 32 (April 1922), 71.

21. In this respect it is interesting to note that Pendleton's Lithography in Boston printed advertisements for several businesses in Charleston, South Carolina. Examples are in the American Antiquarian Society collection.

22. Information on Maverick is derived from Peters, *America On Stone*, 273–275; and Stephen DeWhitt Stephens, *The Mavericks, American Engravers* (New Brunswick, NJ: Rutgers University Press, 1950).

23. Editors' notices of Imbert's press appeared in the *New-York Evening Post* for October 15, 1825, and the *New-York American* for November 9, 1825. See John Carbonell, "Anthony Imbert, New York's Pioneer Lithographer," in *Prints and Printmakers of New York State, 1825–1940*, ed. David Tatham (Syracuse, NY: Syracuse University Press, 1986), 12. Carbonell is the main source for information on Imbert.

24. Information on Imbert prior to his arrival in New York is supplied in the description of the "Lithographical Department" in Cadwallader D. Colden, *Memoir… Presented to the Mayor of the City, at the Celebration of the Completion of the New York Canals* (New York: 1825), 358. Although the publication date is 1825, the lithographs and text of the *Memoir* were not completed until the summer of 1826.

25. Carbonell, 24–5; 40, n. 16. Imbert paid Davis for the views and undertook the printing and publishing at his own expense.

26. Carbonell maintains that American connoisseurs were biased toward European works and failed to patronize native art even when of high quality (p.25).

27. Desobry's name appears on the title page to the Davis/Imbert *Views of Public Buildings* series. See Carbonell, 40, n. 16.

28. Information on Desobry is derived from Peters, *America on Stone*, 157–8.

29. Advertisements in the *New York Evening Post* for October 19 and November 16, 1826, are cited in Carbonell, 40–41, n. 18. Carbonell (p.26) refers to Fleetwood's music publishing.

30. Fleetwood's New York business continued until 1848 when he moved to Cincinnati, where he headed the lithographic firm of Fleetwood & Son. He drew on stone as well as printed, and in later years his output included buildings and views as well as music. See Peters, *America On Stone*, 188–9; and George C. Groce and David H. Wallace, *The New-York Historical Society's Dictionary of Artists in America, 1564–1860* (New Haven: Yale University Press, 1957).

31. Information on the Pendletons is derived from David Tatham, "The Pendleton-Moore Shop. Lithographic Artists in Boston, 1825–1840," *Old Time New England*, 62 (Fall 1971), 29–46; Taylor, "Some Notes," 71–76; and Sally Pierce and Catharina Slautterback, *Boston Lithography, 1825–1880, The Boston Athenæum Collection* (Boston: The Boston Athenæum, 1991), 3–8, 146–148.

32. Mabel M. Swan, "The American Kings," *Antiques*, 19 (April 1931), 278–281, gives a complete account of this confusing project.

33. Taylor, "Some Notes," 75. Thaxter intended to lithograph circulars, but had trouble operating the press.

34. Advertisements for these prints appeared in the *Boston Daily Advertiser*, August 20, 1825, p. 3, col. 6, and August 31, 1825, p. 3 col. 6; and the *Independent Chronicle and Boston Patriot*, August 24, 1825, p. 3 col. 5, and August 31, 1825, p. 3 col. 5.

35. Fred B. Adelson, "Home on La Grange: Alvan Fisher's Lithographs of Lafayette's Residence in France," *Antiques*, 134 (July 1988), 156, quotes from an entry in Fisher's diary saying that they called on "Mr. Milbart." While in France, Fisher did a series of paintings of Lafayette's home, had them copied on stone by Deroy and printed at the press of Villain; he brought them back to Boston to be published by himself in 1826.

36. A notice in the *Columbian Centinel*, November 16, 1825, quoted in Swan, 179.

37. Letter from John Doggett & Co., to Mr. Salmon Brown, May 8, 1829, quoted in Swan, 281. Each print cost $2.00, with an additional charge of fifty cents if printed on India paper.

38. Ibid.

39. Bowen's copy of Engelmann is in the American Antiquarian Society collection.

40. *Boston News-Letter*, February 4, 1826, quoted in Taylor, "Some Notes," 72.

41. *The Court of Death* was exhibited at Doggett's Repository in May 1821. See Lillian B. Miller, *In Pursuit of Fame: Rembrandt Peale 1778–1860* (Washington, DC: National Portrait Gallery, Smithsonian Institution, 1992), 141.

42. An inscribed and dated impression is in the American Antiquarian Society collection.

43. Information on Lucas and his partner Kennedy is derived from Nicholas B. Wainwright, *Philadelphia in the Romantic Age of Lithography* (1958; reprint Philadelphia: Historical Society of Pennsylvania, 1970), 9–10, 25–26.

44. An advertisement in the *National Gazette*, December 9 and 10, 1828, announced their business: "Kennedy & Lucas inform the public they have established their Press at No. 90 south Third, where specimens can be seen. Artists and Amateurs can be supplied with chalk and stone." Quoted in Wainwright, 10.

45. Information on Childs and his partnerships is from Wainwright, 10–29.

46. *United States Gazette*, September 9, 1828, quoted in Wainwright, 13.

47. "Albert Newsam — The Deaf and Dumb Orphan Boy," *American Turf Register and Sporting Magazine*, 1 (January 1830), 253–254. For a full account of Newsam's career see Wendy Wick Reaves, "Portraits for Every Parlor. Albert Newsam and American Portrait Lithography," in *American Portrait Prints. Proceedings of the Tenth Annual American Print Conference*, edited by Wendy Wick Reaves (Charlottesville: University Press of Virginia for the National Portrait Gallery, Smithsonian Institution, 1984), 83–134.

48. Peters, *America On Stone*, facing p. 32, displays an advertising bill head for Pendleton in New York, dated 1829.

49. Wainwright, 14.

50. Although John Pendleton was directing his energies elsewhere, the co-partnership of W. & J. Pendleton was not formally dissolved until March 9, 1831. See notice in *Boston Daily Advertiser*, March 15, 1831, p. 1 col. 5.

51. Information on the Senefelder firm is derived from Pierce and Slautterback, *Boston Lithography*, 150–151; Taylor, "Some Notes," 76–77; and Pamela Hoyle, "The Senefelder Press, 1828–1838," unpublished notes to the exhibition "A Sampling of Four Boston Lithographers," held at the Boston Athenæum in February 1979.

52. William W. Clapp, Jr., *A Record of the Boston Stage* (Boston and Cambridge: James Munroe and Company, 1853), 263–264. Mrs. Ware contributed an address for the opening night of the Tremont Theatre's 1828 season.

53. Announcements of the contest appeared in *Bower of Taste*, 1 (19 April 1828), 254; and 1 (July 5, 1828), 430. The story and illustration were published in 1 (July 12, 1828).

54. For notices of the drawing book and a portrait of Dr. Freeman see *Bower of Taste*, 1 (December 13, 1828), 798; for portraits of Dr. Gorham after a painting by Williams, and Josiah Quincy after Stuart see 2 (July 11, 1829), 445.

55. *Bower of Taste*, 1 (March 22, 1828), 190.

56. The oft repeated statement that William Pendleton absorbed the Senefelder press in 1831 originates from Taylor, "Some Notes," 76. Taylor derived much of his information from interviews with John W. A. Scott (1815–1907), who had begun working for Pendleton ca. 1831. See Tatham, "The Pendleton-Moore Shop," 35, 46, n. 21.

57. Dixon's annotated trial lithographs and a research file on them are in the American Antiquarian Society collection. Dixon went on to explore medicine, chemistry, and optics. He experimented with the daguerreotype and pursued photography and photolithography. Many of us use pencils manufactured by a company he founded.

58. *Baltimore Patriot and Mercantile Advertiser* for April 7, 1830. For information on Endicott & Swett see Georgia Brady Bumgardner, "George and William Endicott: Commercial Lithography in New York, 1831–51," in *Prints and Printmakers of New York State, 1825–1940,* ed. David Tatham (Syracuse, NY: Syracuse University Press, 1986), 44–46.

59. "A CARD" in the *Boston Daily Advertiser,* March 17, 1831, p. 2, col. 6, places Harvey at Graphic Court and announces his intention to visit Europe.

60. A notice in the *Baltimore American,* March 13, 1827, quoted in John A. Mahey, "Lithographs by Rembrandt Peale," *Antiques,* 97 (February 1970), 237, names the lithographs sold at the Peale Museum. A. J. Davis exhibited lithographs at the National Academy of Design in 1828 and 1829, alongside paintings and architectural designs. See *National Academy of Design Exhibition Record, 1826–1860.* 2 vols. (New York: Printed for the New-York Historical Society, 1943), 1: 114.

61. Michael Twyman, "Lithographic Stone and the Printing Trade in the Nineteenth Century," *Journal of the Printing Historical Society,* 8 (1972), 24–26.

62. Quoted in Katharine Minot Channing, comp., *Minot Family Letters, 1773–1871* (Sherborn, Mass.: Privately Printed, 1957), 263. Minot, the wife of a Boston lawyer, was taught lithography by John Pendleton. She later taught drawing in the Boston schools and wrote two books on perspective, published in 1830 and 1841. For biographical information on Minot see Channing, 203; and *A Genealogical Record of the Minot Family in America and England* (Boston: Privately Printed, 1897), 41.

63. The Derby album is in the Print Room, Boston Athenæum.

64. The Quincy scrapbooks are in the Rare Book Room, Boston Public Library. I am grateful to Sinclair Hitchings for bringing them to my attention. The volume under discussion is vol. 7, 1830–1836, although it contains work dated earlier and later, and shows signs of having been amended after its initial compilation. Two of the newspaper clippings relate to lithography: the story of Senefelder's invention, p. 46; and an account from Brussels of a transfer method for printing text, p. 94.

65. Quincy scrapbooks, v. 7, facing p. 34. The small view of a European style house in a lane surrounded by trees and a wall, is inscribed: "Drawn on Stone by Eliza S. Quincy, 1826."

66. Quincy scrapbooks, v. 7. Colman's *House of Colonel Pickman* [*Salem*], printed by Pendleton's, is inserted in the front of the scrapbook; *Rev. H. Colman's Church, Salem,* printed by Senefelder's, is facing p. 119; Susan Cabot's *Samuel,* after Sir Joshua Reynolds, printed by Pendleton's, faces p. 47.

67. *Boston Daily Advertiser,* March 24, 1825, p. 2, col. 1.

68. "Valuable French Prints," *Boston Daily Advertiser,* March 25, 1825, p. 3, col. 5, reflects the popular taste. It lists: "sets of Engravings from Wilkie, Burnet, Westall, and others; Scripture Pieces; Classical Subjects; Landscapes, plain and colored; Theatrical Costumes; Heads; Grimaces; Caricatures; Views of cities and Public Buildings; Subjects of Devotion; Portraits of Distinguished Females; Views and Scenes in Paris, . . ."

69. For example, in the *Boston Daily Advertiser,* November 13, 1830, p. 3 col. 1, Pendleton's advertised copies of Henry Inman's portrait of Clara Fisher, the popular comic actress. This was probably the stipple and aquatint engraving executed in New York by Stephen Henry Gimber and William James Bennett and dedicated to the actress by the New York publisher, G. M. Bourne. Imported prints were advertised in the *Boston Daily Advertiser,* November 11, 1830, p. 3, col. 3: "LITHOGRAPHS RECEIVED by the *Wolga,* from Havre, the greatest variety of PRINTS ever imported by the subscribers [W. & J. Pendleton], which they offer wholesale and retail at moderate prices. The collection embraces many beautiful Portraits, — Landscapes, and Fancy Pieces — Flowers, Fruits, and Butterflies, richly coloured — and a great number of small prints suitable for Scraps." Music in several languages, "all on beautiful tinted paper, and in Bourne's best style," was advertised as "NEW MUSIC," *Boston Daily Advertiser,* November 13, 1830, p. 3, col. 1.

70. "Byron Circulating Library," *Boston Daily Advertiser,* February 23, 1831, p. 2, col. 6, advertised "an elegant assortment of Lithographic Prints, Engravings and Scraps."

71. *National Gazette and Literary Register,* May 28, 1827, p. 3.

72. Carbonell, "Anthony Imbert," 24–25, discusses Bourne as a print seller. Hobson advertised "LITHOGRAPHIC portraits of Robert Owen, Lord Byron, Hannah Moore [*sic*] &c. for sale," *National Gazette and Literary Register,* June 23, 1827, p. 3.

73. An advertisement for "NEW MUSIC" lists examples of "Bourne's beautiful plate music, tinted paper and Vignette Titles" for sale at the Pendleton shop. See *Boston Daily Advertiser,* January 8, 1831, p. 3, col. 1.

74. "Literary Novelties," *National Gazette and Literary Register,* July 26, 1825, p. 2.

75. Ibid.

76. William Robert Prince, *Treatise on the Vine* (New York: T. & J. Swords and others, 1830), dedication addressed to Henry Clay of Kentucky. See cat. 76.

EARLY AMERICAN LITHOGRAPHY

Images to 1830

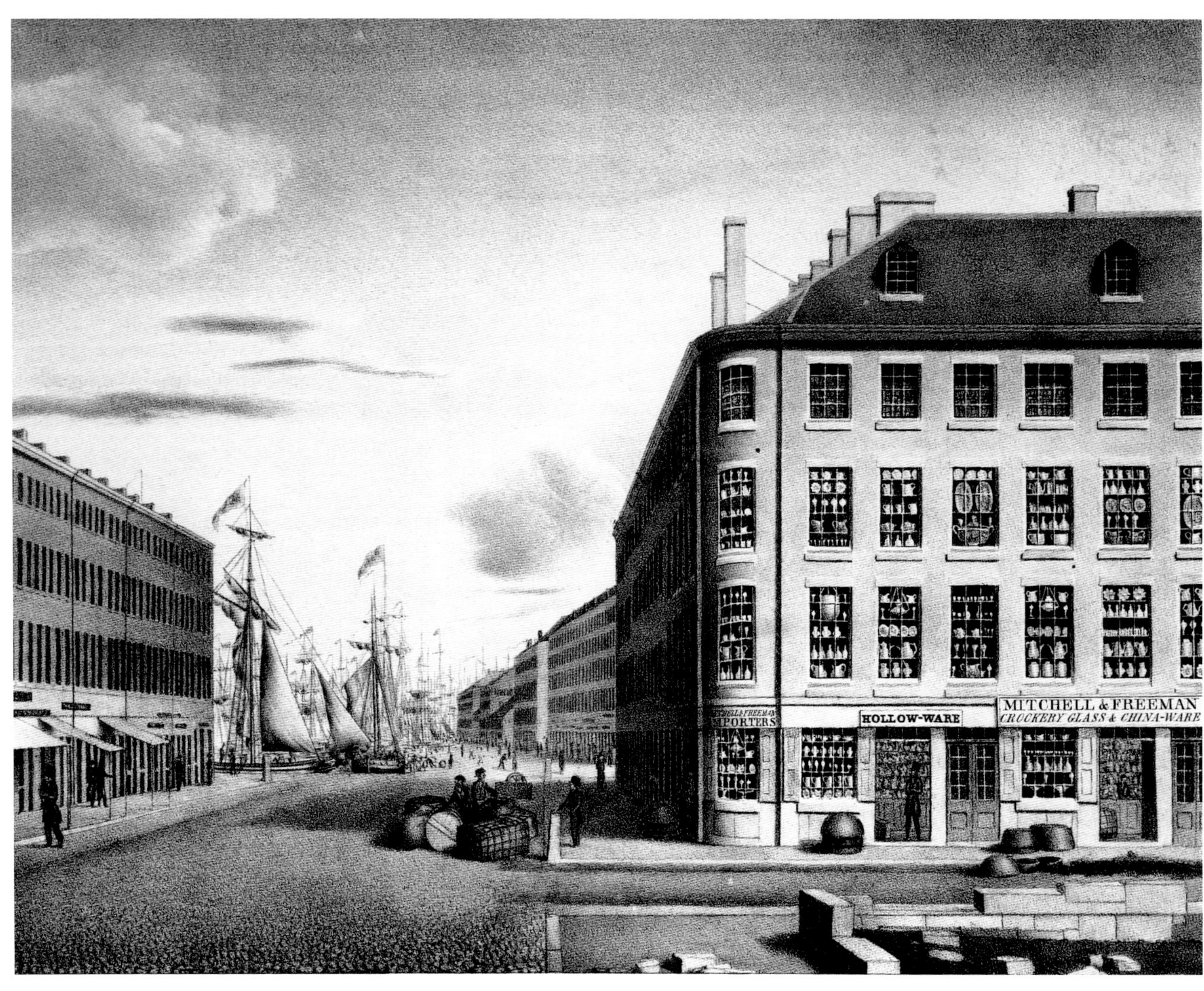

Cat. 1 Anonymous, *Mitchell & Freeman's China, Crockery & Glass-Warehouse, Boston* (ca. 1828–1831).

26

PRINTS

Dimensions are rounded to the quarter inch and include image and printed text; height precedes width.

Anonymous.

1 **Mitchell & Freeman's China, Crockery & Glass Warehouse / Chatham St., Boston.**
Crayon lithograph on wove paper, ca. 1828–1831. 9½ x 11 in. Printed on stone l.r.: *Pendletons Lithography Boston.*
Boston Athenæum; by exchange, 1994.

The Mitchell & Freeman shop was established in 1825 and moved to its new warehouse at 12 Chatham Street in 1828.[1] As importers of fancy crockware, the shop's proximity to Long Wharf was ideal. This lithograph shows Long Wharf in the distance with its shipping vessels and rows of warehouses and shops. Long Wharf, built in 1710, extended nearly 800 feet into the harbor, and allowed for the direct packing and unpacking of the largest shipping vessels. The lively wharf scene illustrated in this lithograph accurately depicts the enormous vitality of Boston Harbor in the late 1820s, during which time an average 787 foreign vessels and nearly 3,000 coasting vessels landed each year in Boston.

This lithograph may have been commissioned as an advertisement for the Mitchell & Freeman firm. An impression of this print was obtained by the celebrated English potter, William Adams of Stoke-upon-Trent, who reproduced the view on ten-inch plates of Staffordshire china. The plates were produced in blue and the view was surrounded by an elaborate border of leaves and branches.[2] Undoubtedly the firm of Mitchell & Freeman would have been pleased to sell these plates in their store.
C. S.

Anonymous.

2 **Trenton Falls.**
Transfer lithograph on wove paper, ca. 1827.
8 x 11¼ in. Printed on stone l.l.: *Imbert's litho. transfer* [New York City].
American Antiquarian Society.

This unsigned lithograph was produced by the transfer process. Rather than draw directly on stone, an artist could make a drawing on paper which was then transferred to the stone, eliminating the necessity of reversing the image. Imbert's firm produced a number of transfer lithographs by John Robert Murray (1775–1851), an ama-

teur artist. Another print by Murray, a scene of cows and sheep in a stream, has a similar softness of tone.[3]

Trenton Falls, situated just fourteen miles north of Utica, New York, was a favorite tourist attraction beginning in the early 1800s. The main fall was ninety feet in height; others were less high, but still powerful, particularly after a rain storm. In 1823 the Reverend John Sherman opened a small inn at Trenton Falls, the Rural Retreat, where people could rest or spend the night. In 1827 he published the first of seven pamphlets extolling the scenery, writing: "We have in effect the peerless majesty, the awful power, and the deep volleying thunder of the grand cataract of Niagara, which causes the heavens to shake and the earth to tremble; which forces the son of pride to feel himself mere insignificance on the verge of annihilation."[4] Artists who visited the Falls before 1830 include Thomas Doughty, James P. Cockburn, Auguste Guerber, Jacques G. Milbert, Samuel F. B. Morse and Catherine Scollay.   G. B.

Anonymous (after H. Corbin Kidder [1801–1874]).

3 **View of Amherst College, Mass. from the President's House.**
Crayon lithograph with hand-coloring on wove paper, ca. 1827–1828. 8¼ x 12¾ in. Printed on stone l.l.: *H C. Kidder pinxt.;* l.r.: *Pendletons Litho.* [Boston].
Boston Athenæum.

Originally known as the Collegiate Charitable Institution of Amherst, Amherst College was founded in 1821 to provide a liberal education for "pious and indigent men"[5] who wished to enter the Christian ministry. The reputation of the College grew rapidly and it was soon esteemed the equal, if not the superior, of Yale and Harvard. The student population soared, and by the mid-1820s the College was forced to expand physically.

In the February 5, 1828, edition of the *Boston Patriot and Mercantile Advertiser,* the following announcement of this print appeared: "Amherst College. A beautiful lithographic print giving a view of this institution has just been published by Pendleton. The view presents five edifices on a line, fronting the west. We understand that only the three central buildings are completed, but the fourth is commenced and the fifth will be erected soon to furnish accommodations for the increasing number of students, already amounting to 210." The print was originally accompanied by text describing Amherst College and its desirability.[6] The lithograph depicts Johnson Chapel, the central building, and to the left, a dormitory known as North, or Middle, College.

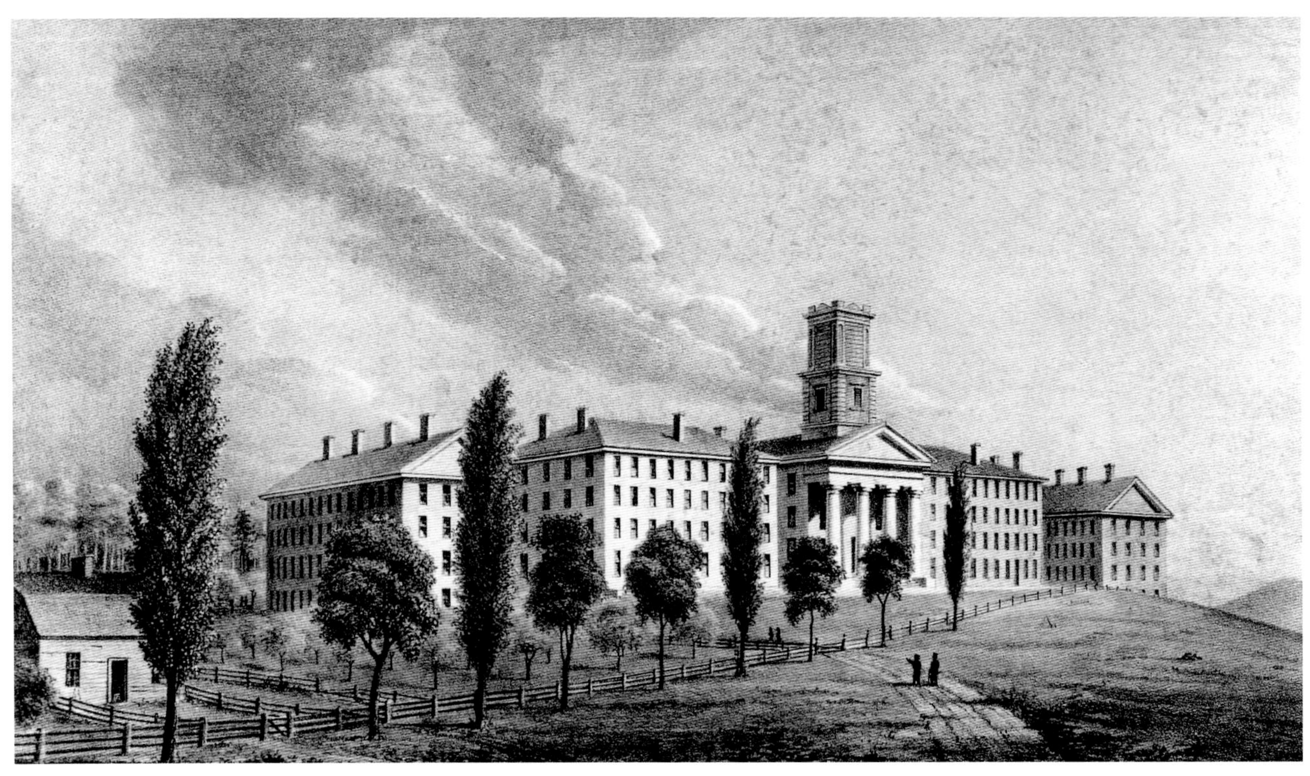

Cat. 3   Anonymous, after H. Corbin Kidder, *View of Amherst College, Mass.* (ca. 1827–1828).

The buildings did not inspire universal admiration. Edward Hitchcock, Professor of Geology and later President of the College from 1844 to 1854, thought the buildings lacked any architectural merit. He wrote: "They form an unsightly row of brick and mortar — mere hollow parallelopipeds [*sic*] divided into compartments called rooms." He consoled himself, however, with the reminder that "to prepare men for the Christian ministry was the grand object [of the college], and every thing not essential to this was conscientiously avoided."[7]

One of those young men was the artist of this composition. H. Corbin Kidder, class of 1828, was a self-taught, but highly talented, artist. While a student at Amherst, he painted portraits of the college president and several of his fellow students. He abandoned his decision to become an artist when the religious revivals swept through Amherst in 1827 and 1828, and "renouncing his infidel sentiments," he gave up his art work and entered the ministry, graduating from Andover Theological Seminary in 1832.[8]   C. S.

Washington Blanchard (1808–1855).
4. **William E. Channing, D. D.**
Crayon lithograph on wove paper, 1830. 12 x 8¾ in. Printed on stone l.l.: *Chester Harding Pinxt.;* l.c.: *on stone by W. Blanchard;* l.r.: *Pendleton's Lithography, Boston.*
Boston Athenæum; gift of Charles E. Mason, Jr., 1977.

In 1827–1828, Chester Harding (1792–1866) painted a portrait of the forty-eight year-old William Ellery Channing (1780–1842), America's preeminent liberal theologian and pastor of Boston's Federal Street Church. Harding's studio was located then at 16 Beacon Street. Eliza Susan Quincy visited his studios and later commented: ". . . How well I remember both his studios. The first was in Beacon Street, near the present Athenæum — I can see the portraits ranged on the floor, for they succeeded each other so rapidly that there was no time to frame and hang them . . ."[9] Harding apparently found time to frame the portrait of Reverend Channing, for it was exhibited at the Athenæum's Gallery in 1828 with Channing cited as the owner. The oil portrait has since disappeared but, fortunately, it was replicated in lithographic form by the Boston miniature painter Washington Blanchard. An advertisement for the print appeared in the February 10, 1831, edition of the *Boston Daily Advertiser:* "PORTRAITS OF DR. CHANNING — For sale by L. C. Bowles, No. 124 Washington Street. — Lythrographic [*sic*] Prints of Rev. Wm. E. Channing, D. D., from a painting by Harding. Price $1."

Chester Harding once noted that portraiture was "that branch of the fine arts which depends mainly upon the vanity of mankind for its support."[10] It is doubtful that he had Rev. Channing in mind when he made this remark, but Channing could not fail to be aware of his own enormous influence. At the time this portrait was made, he was writing a two-part article for the *Christian Examiner* entitled "Life and Character of Napoleon Bonaparte," in which he made the following observation: "The energy which is to carry forward the intellect of a people, belongs chiefly to private individuals, who devote themselves to lonely thought, who worship truth, who originate the views demanded by their age, who help us to throw off the yoke of established prejudices, who improve old modes of education or invent better . . ."[11] A truer description of Channing himself could scarcely be made.   C. S.

Mannevillette Elihu Dearing Brown (1810–1896).
5 **[In Memoria].**
Crayon lithograph on wove paper, ca. 1827–1830. 9¾ x 12½ in. Printed on stone l.r.: *M. E. D. Brown delt.;* l.c.: *Pub.d & sold at W. & J. Pendleton's Estab.t No. 1 Graphic Court Boston;* l.r.: *Pendleton's Lithog. Boston.*
Boston Athenæum purchase, 1979.

"Mourning pictures" were extremely popular in nineteenth-century America and were produced in a wide variety of media — watercolors, embroidered needlework, miniatures, and prints. Often they were framed and mounted on the wall as a permanent reminder of the deceased. The number of surviving "mourning prints" suggests that they were a mainstay of many lithographic firms. Typically, the gravestone on the print was left blank so the owner could inscribe the name and dates of the deceased along with a Biblical quotation or an epitaph.

The composition and symbols in M. E. D. Brown's *In Memoria* is characteristic of most early to mid-nineteenth-century "mourning pictures," combining neoclassical emblems with a romantic sensibility. A gravestone with a Grecian urn and a grieving woman in classical dress are situated in the foreground. To the left is a weeping willow, a common symbol of mourning, and on the right is a large and healthy oak, a tree traditionally associated with strength and long life. In the background is a tranquil landscape with a mountain and a calm lake. These distant landscapes — so ubiquitous in "mourning pictures" — were not just an artistic means of providing perspective. To the viewer they may well have suggested both the separation from the loved one and the deceased's peaceful future life.

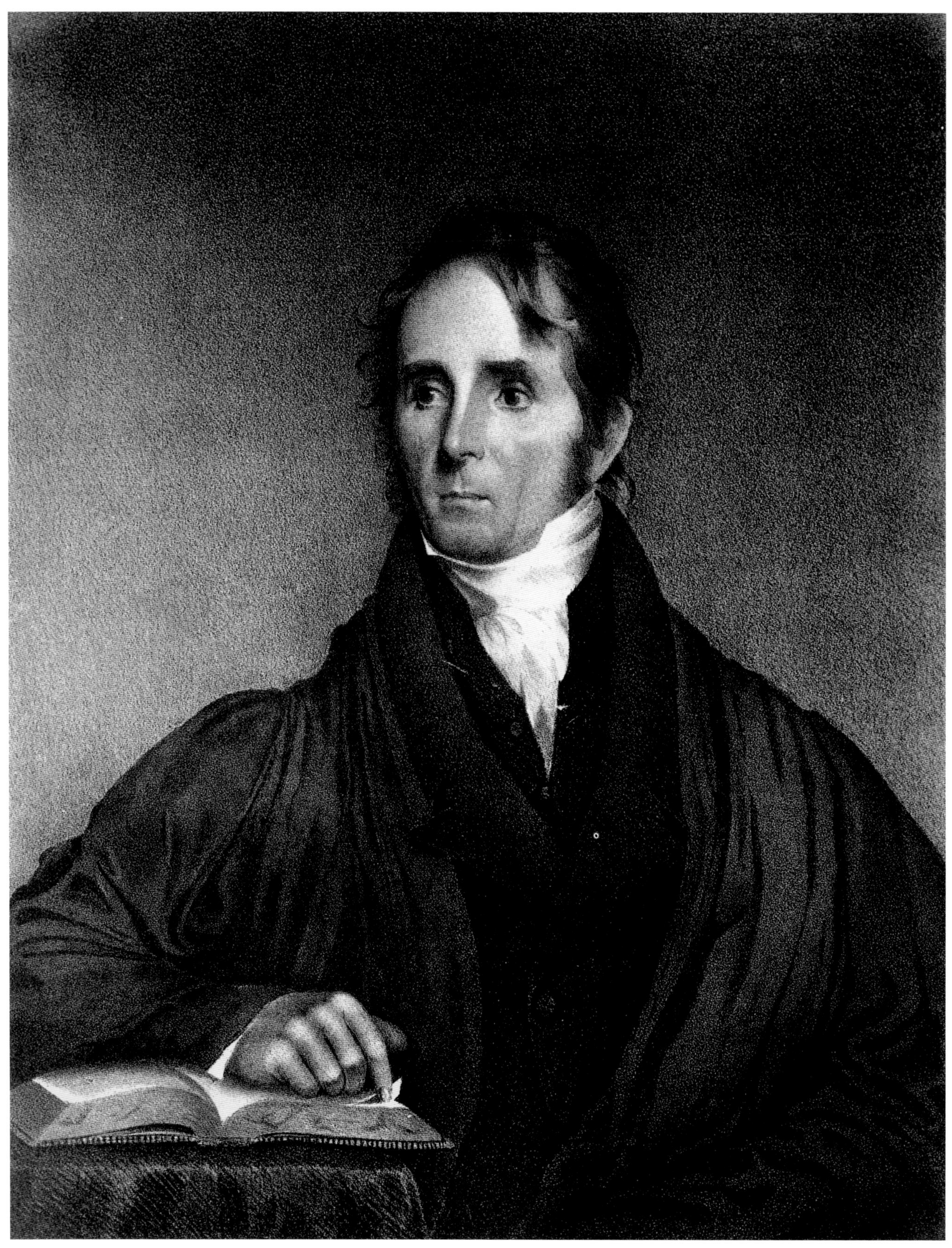

Cat. 4   Washington Blanchard, *William E. Channing, D. D.* (1830).

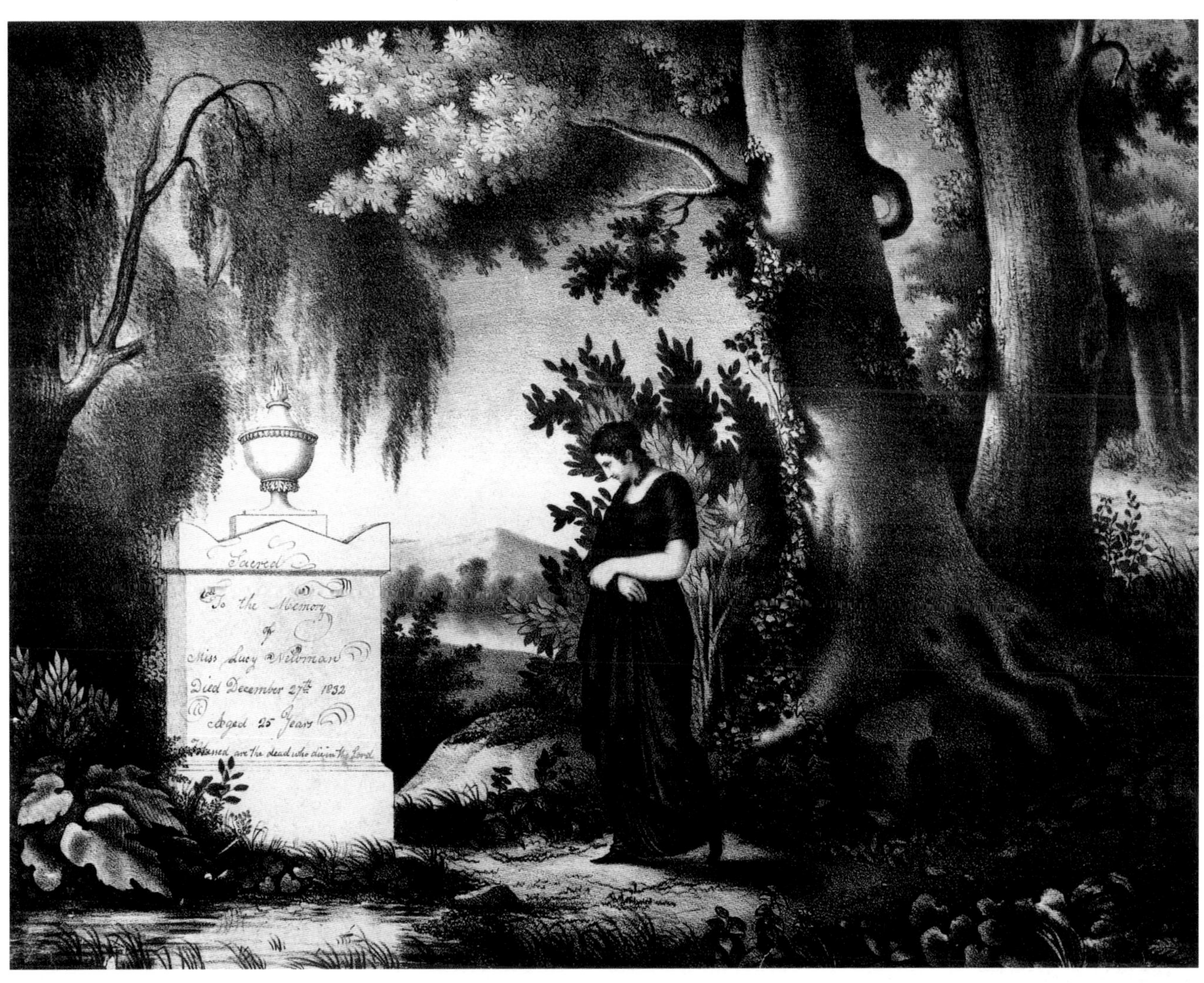

Cat. 5 M. E. D. Brown, [*In Memoria*] (ca. 1827–1830).

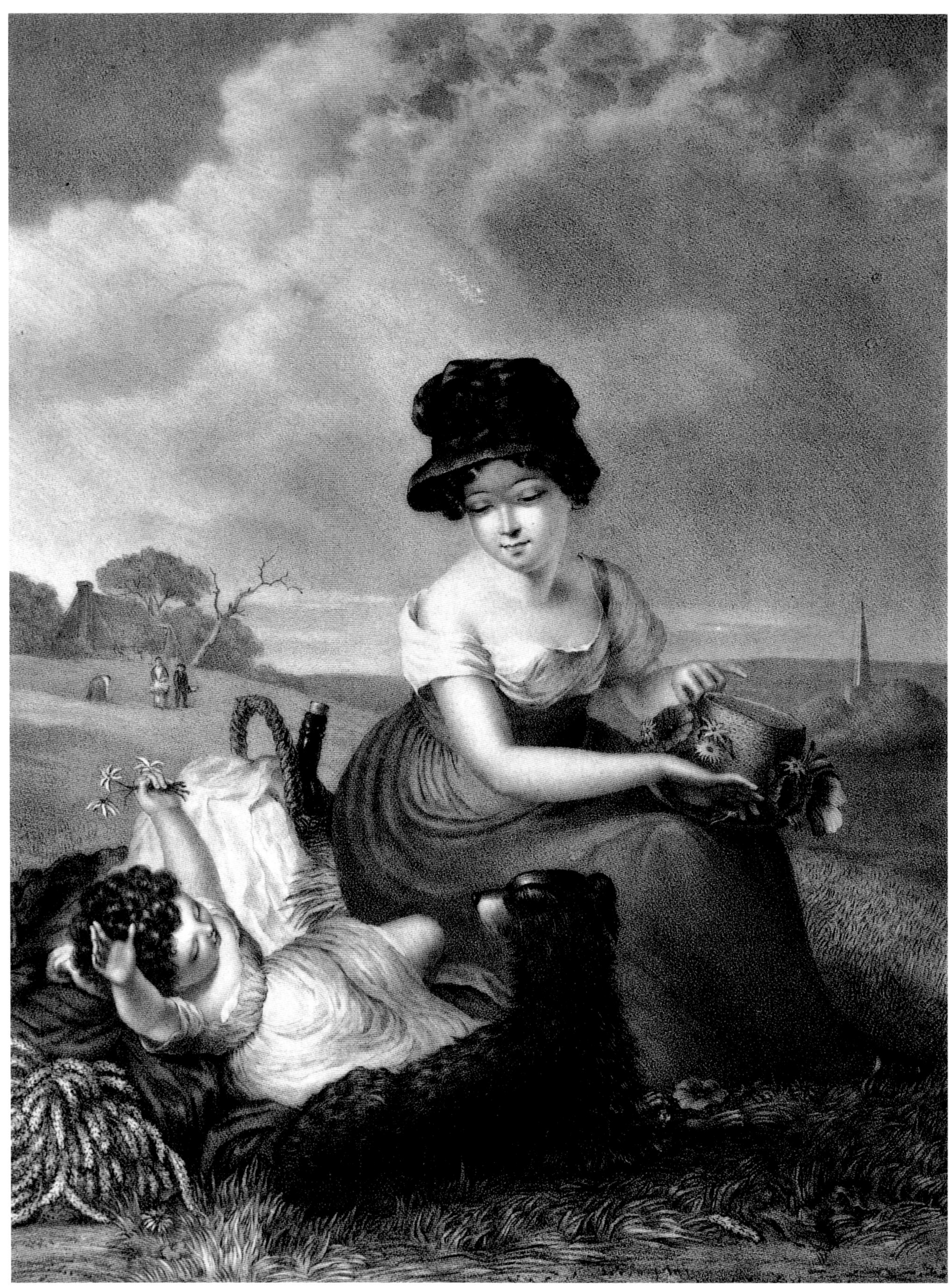

Cat. 6   M. E. D. Brown, *The Rustic Wreath* (ca. 1828–1831).

The inscription on this lithograph's tombstone reads: *Sacred / to the Memory / of / Miss Lucy Newman / Died December 27th 1832 / Aged 25 years / Blessed are the dead who die in The Lord.*   C. S.

Mannevillette Elihu Dearing Brown (1810–1896).
6   The Rustic Wreath.
Crayon lithograph on white wove paper, ca. 1828–1831. 13 x 9 in. Printed on stone l.l.: *W. F. Witherington Pinxt.;* l.r.: *Drawn on stone by M. E. D. Brown.* Printed on stone on attached paper beneath caption: *Printed & Published at Pendleton's Lithographic Estab.t Boston.* Boston Athenæum purchase, 1983.

The original painting for this lithograph was created by the British landscape artist William Frederick Witherington (1785–1865), and exhibited at the British Institution in 1828. Since there is no record that M. E. D. Brown ever visited England, it is likely that he copied this image from an engraving of the painting. Genre scenes such as these were extremely popular throughout the nineteenth century and could be found on the walls of many American homes.

Witherington was elected to the Royal Academy in 1830 and had a long and prolific career. *The Rustic Wreath* is characteristic of his picturesque painting style; he had a penchant for sentimental, pastoral British scenes populated with idealized "rustic" figures. Occasionally he depicted scenes from contemporary literature.

Upon his death, the *Art Journal* wrote "The works of this artist will never take rank in the highest class of English landscape painting . . . but . . . [he] is a true lover of English ground, and an able illustrator of its 'thousand sights of loveliness.'"[12]   C. S.

John Cheney (1801–1885).
7   [Trade card for W. & J. Pendleton].
Crayon lithograph on wove paper, 1827–1830. 3¾ x 2½ in. Printed on stone l.c.: *J. Cheney — on stone* [Boston].
American Antiquarian Society.

John Cheney taught himself to engrave and even constructed a printing press on his own. He moved from Connecticut to Boston in 1826 and found employment in the Pendleton firm as a lithographic artist, and in the early 1830s he and his brother Seth, also a noted engraver, studied painting in London and Paris. Upon his return to the United States in 1835, he worked as an engraver, producing elegant plates for various book publishers in New York, Philadelphia, and Boston.

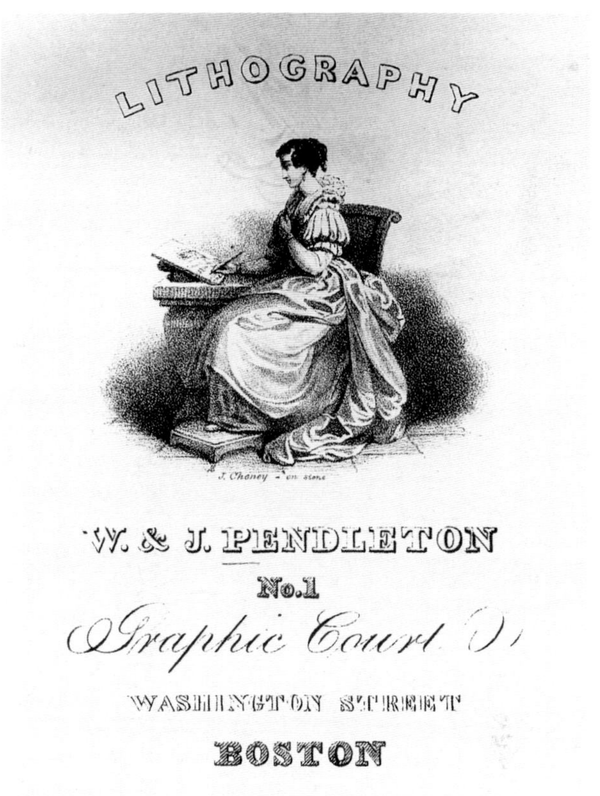

Cat. 7   John Cheney, *Trade card for W. & J. Pendleton* (ca. 1827–1830).

This advertisement for the Pendleton firm, copied from a vignette on the title page of C. H. Hullmandel's *The Art of Drawing on Stone,* is noteworthy for its image of a woman drawing on a lithographic stone. Lithographic firms in the 1820s and 1830s sought to attract amateur artists to their shops and made their equipment available to them. A number of women made use of this practice in Boston — Mary Jane Derby, Eliza Goodridge, Louisa Minot, Catherine Scollay, and Margaret Clark Snow were among the most active and skilled.   G. B.

Cephas G. Childs (1793–1871).
8   [Proof for *The Cabinet*].
Crayon lithograph on India paper, 1829. 4 x 3½ in. Printed on stone l.c.: *on stone. Childs, Direx. / J. Laval & S. F. Bradford. / Printed by P. K. & C. Philada.* American Antiquarian Society; gift of Charles Henry Taylor.

The Cabinet is an early example of the genre known as "literary annuals," elegantly illustrated and bound books designed to be presented as gifts at Christmas time. The

format of gift books was generally small, so the lithographed illustrations were often murky because artists
and draftsmen found it difficult to use the lithographic
crayon successfully on such a small scale. This proof for
the title page of *The Cabinet* is a noteworthy exception —
the drawing is particularly sharp and crisp.   G. B.

Cephas G. Childs (1793–1871).

9   The White Plume.
Crayon lithograph with scratching out and *tusche* on
wove paper, 1830. 12¼ x 7¾ in. Printed on stone l.c.:
*Philadelphia. Published by C. G. Childs. 80 Walnut
Street 1830. / on Stone. C. G. Childs Lithr.*
American Antiquarian Society; gift of Charles Henry
Taylor.

Copied from *La Reverie,* a French print, *The White Plume*
presents a beautiful young woman stylishly posed and
dressed. The solid black rim of her *chapeau* and the bodice
of her dress contrast with the white feathers and her pale
skin tones. A different version of the print, which presented
the figure on a balcony overlooking a landscape, was
issued by the firm of Anthony Imbert in New York about
1827.[13] A contemporary newspaper notice of *The White
Plume* reported that *The White Plume* and another lithograph by Childs exemplified "the great progress which
this truly useful art is making in this country."[14]   G. B.

Cephas G. Childs (1793–1871), attrib.

10   The Natural Bridge.
Crayon lithograph on wove paper, ca. 1830. 9½ x 6¾
in. Printed on stone l.c.: *PHILADELPHIA / Pub.
By C. G. Childs 80 Walnut Street.*
American Antiquarian Society; gift of Charles Henry
Taylor.

Although the plate is not signed, we can attribute it to
Cephas G. Childs, the publisher. Considered one of
America's great attractions, the Natural Bridge was
depicted by European and American artists beginning in
the early 1780s. The Natural Bridge, still a popular tourist
attraction, is in Virginia, west of Richmond in
Rockbridge County. Childs achieves a sense of scale by
including a figure at the lower right, sketching in a note-
book. The contrast between the dark shaded cliff on the
left and the sunstruck cliff on the right makes this a particularly successful depiction.   G. B.

Thomas Cole (1801–1848).

**11   Distant View of the Slides That Destroyed the
Whilley Family. White Mountains.**
Crayon lithograph on wove paper, ca. 1828.
9½ x 11 in. Printed on stone l.l.: *Cole delt.;*
l.r.: *Imbert's Lithography* [New York City].
American Antiquarian Society.

The well-known Hudson River painter, Thomas Cole,
produced at least three lithographed prints, probably in
1828. His first trip to the White Mountains of New
Hampshire occurred in 1827, when he and fellow artist
Henry Cheever Pratt (1803–1880) visited the site where
all of the members of the Willey family were killed as
they sought shelter in their barn from a mud slide in the
summer of 1826. The slide destroyed the barn and those
inside it, but their house was left standing. This famous
tragedy actually marked the beginning of the tourist
industry in the White Mountains.

In his diary, Thomas Cole spoke of the swirling clouds
in Crawford Notch, the site of the Willey disaster. Those
swirling clouds can be seen in this lithograph, in which
the destructive forces of nature are depicted in a powerful
and emotional visual language. The fallen trees on the
left and the twisted bare trunk on the right are emblem-
atic of nature's power.   G. B.

James F. Colman (fl. 1828–1831).

**12   [Independent Congregational Church, Barton
Square, Salem, Mass.].**
Crayon lithograph, ca. 1828–1831. 7¼ x 9 in. Printed
on stone l.l.: *J. F. C. Del.;* l.r.: *Senefelder Litho. Co.*
[Boston].
Boston Athenæum purchase, 1993.

The Barton Square Unitarian Church, properly known as
the Independent Congregational Church, was erected in
1824 on Essex Street in Salem, Massachusetts. The architect was Thomas W. Sumner of Brookline; its first minister was Reverend Henry Colman. The establishment of
the church was preceded by a rancorous debate within
the First Church of Salem (Unitarian). Members of the
congregation had offered the position of minister to the
controversial Rev. Colman, a well-known Unitarian
reformer and a former student of Rev. James Freeman.
Colman's opposition to Trinitarianism and to formal religious dogma had earned him the reputation of being a
radical, and his teachings had caused considerable division
within the Salem Unitarian community. Colman's follow-
ers were devoted to him, however, and they decided to

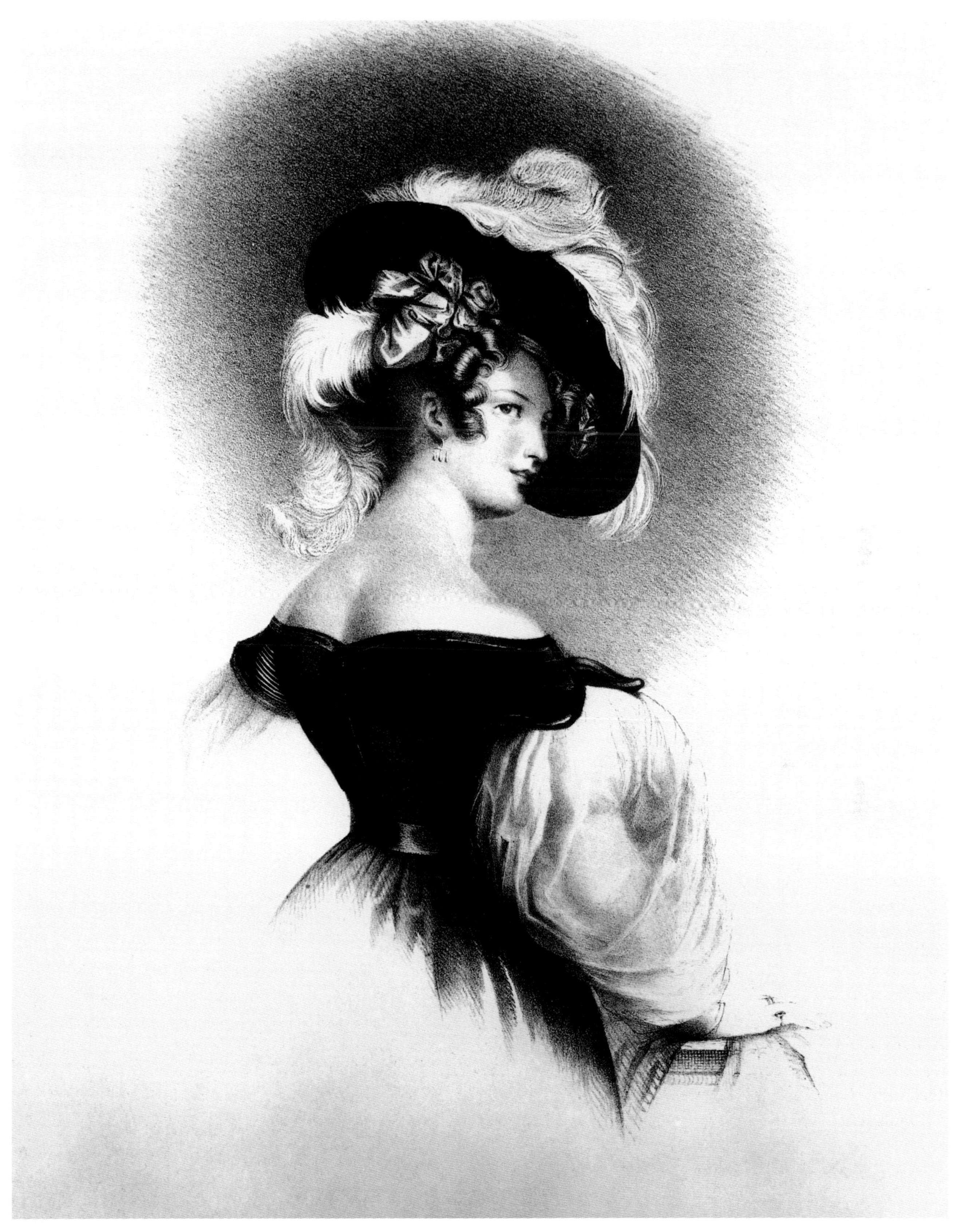

Cat. 9   Cephas G. Childs, *The White Plume* (1830).

form their own church, the Independent Congregational Church, in Barton Square.

Rev. Colman's tenure at the church lasted from 1825 until 1831. Although well-loved by his congregation, his detractors were many and vocal throughout his ministry. The constant disputes, the death of his fourteen-year old daughter in 1830, and his own ill health led him to tender his resignation in December of 1831. Colman "retired" to a farm in Deerfield, Massachusetts, and turned his attention to agricultural matters.[15] The Independent Congregational Church building eventually was made into a theater and destroyed in the early twentieth century.

The Boston Athenæum's impression of this lithograph was part of a scrapbook belonging to the Salem artist Mary Jane Derby (see below), whose family had pews in the Barton Square Unitarian Church during Rev. Colman's tenure. The attribution to James F. Colman is based on a hand-written inscription on an impression in the Rare Book Room of the Boston Public Library.[16] Rev. Colman had five children,[17] one of whom may have been named after his former mentor, Rev. James Freeman. A James Freeman Colman was publishing poetry in Boston in the early 1840s, and the initials "J. F. C." appear on at least one Senefelder and two Pendleton lithographs dating from this period.   c. s.

The ensuing debates were acrimonious and bear a striking resemblance to the controversies surrounding government spending in the 1990s. Mayor Quincy eventually prevailed by assuring Bostonians that the debt would be "temporary" and would improve "the general condition of the city, elevating the character, multiplying its accommodations . . . and patronizing and finding employment for its laborers and mechanics."[19]

Alexander Parris was appointed architect, and the two-story Greek Revival building officially opened on August 26, 1826. Four days later the *Columbian Centinel* observed that "at an early hour all the stalls were occupied and filled with the best produce of the fields . . . and slaughter-houses of our vicinity . . ." The market had 128 stalls on the first floor; the second floor had three large halls which eventually were used for exhibitions and fairs of such organizations as the New England Society for the Promotion of Manufactures and the Mechanic Arts.

Alexander Davis chose to illustrate the west end of Quincy Market. When he drew this scene, the area just east of Quincy Market had not yet been filled, as can be seen from the shipping vessels in the background. In 1828, Davis exhibited a painting of "Market-House, Boston" and a lithograph of the same subject at the National Academy of Design in New York.[20]   c. s.

Alexander Jackson Davis (1803–1892).

13   **Quincy Hall Market Boston.**
Crayon lithograph on wove paper, 1829. 10¼ x 15¼ in. Printed on stone l.l.: *Lith of Pendleton, New York;* l.r.: *A. J. Davis. del & pinxt.*
Boston Athenæum.

Josiah Quincy (1772–1864) was elected mayor of Boston in 1823, and within a month of his inauguration he began to address the problem of cleaning up and enlarging Boston's central market area, Faneuil Hall. By the 1820s, Faneuil Hall was overcrowded, the surrounding streets congested, and many observers commented on its dirty and unsanitary conditions. At the time, Faneuil Hall overlooked the Town Dock, the site of the city's common sewer; it was "a receptacle for every species of filth and a public nuisance . . . [and was] for the most part inhabited by a very troublesome and irregular population."[18]

To deal with the problem, Mayor Quincy proposed filling in the area and building six new streets, a new market house, and two large warehouses east of Faneuil Hall. His plans were considered extravagantly expensive and were met with bitter opposition by citizens and influential members of the City Council and Legislature, who were seriously concerned about government debt.

Alexander Jackson Davis (1803–1892).

14   **State House, Boston.**
Crayon lithograph with hand-coloring on white wove paper, 1827. 14¼ x 18½ in. Inscribed on image l.r.: *104 [?] / 18½* . Printed on stone l.l.: *From measurement by A. J. Davis, A. N. A.;* l.r.: *Lithography of Pendleton Boston.*
Boston Athenæum.

Alexander Davis, a New York architect and artist, arrived in Boston in the late fall of 1827 to study and draw Boston buildings, and arranged with the Pendleton firm to have his drawings made into lithographic prints. He drew approximately twenty-five Boston area edifices and was paid nine dollars per image.

Davis was a friend and disciple of Charles Bulfinch and greatly admired the Massachusetts State House, which had been erected in 1795. It was, in fact, the first building Davis drew in Boston and as, his inscription testifies, he drew it from actual measurements. His view of the State House included the new iron gateway and surrounding fences designed by architect Alexander Parris in 1826.

This Pendleton lithograph was a great success when it was published. In 1834 a critic wrote that the view was "to this day . . . the finest specimen of lithography, in the

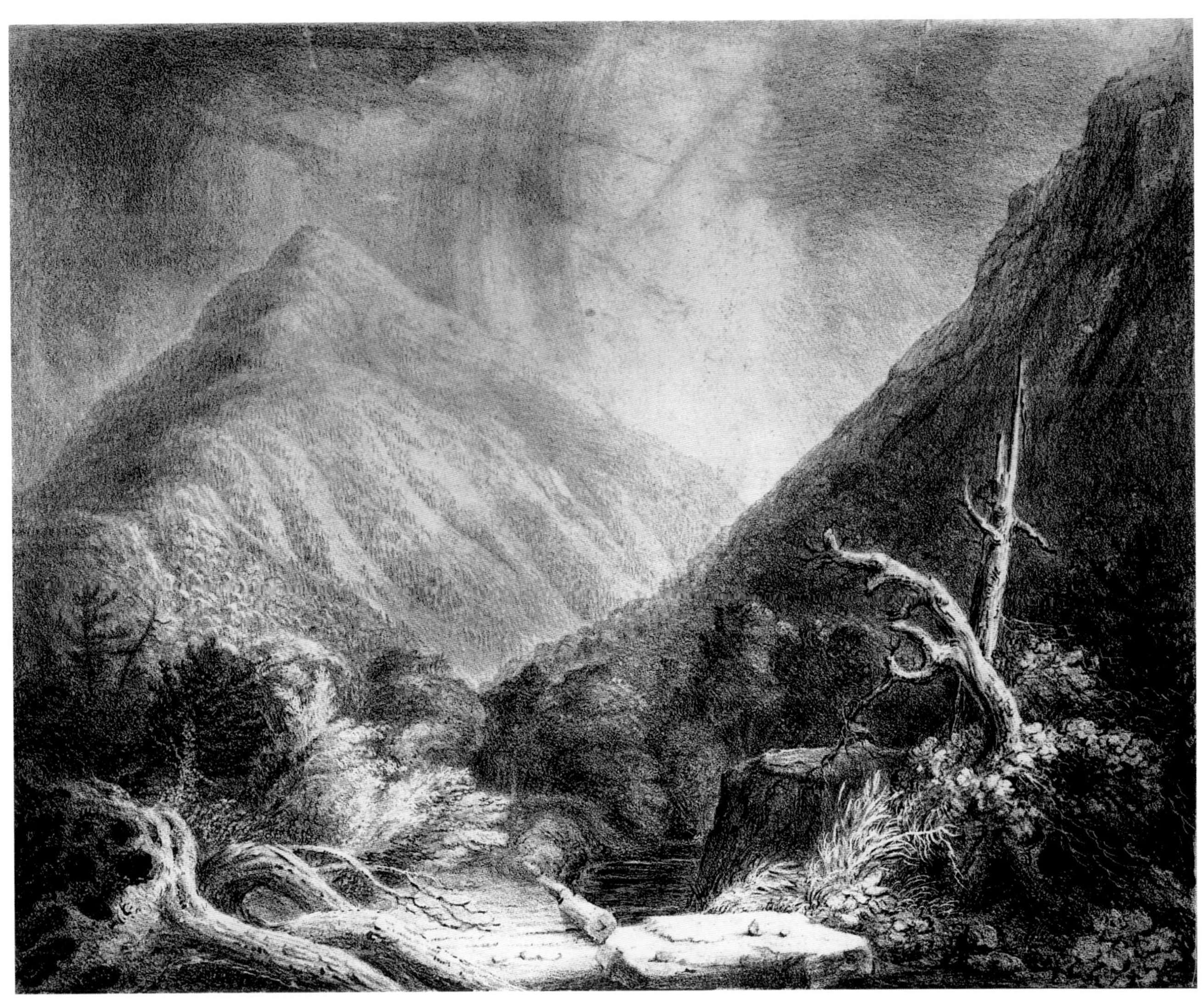

Cat. 11   Thomas Cole, *Distant View of the Slides that Destroyed the Whilley Family* (ca. 1828).

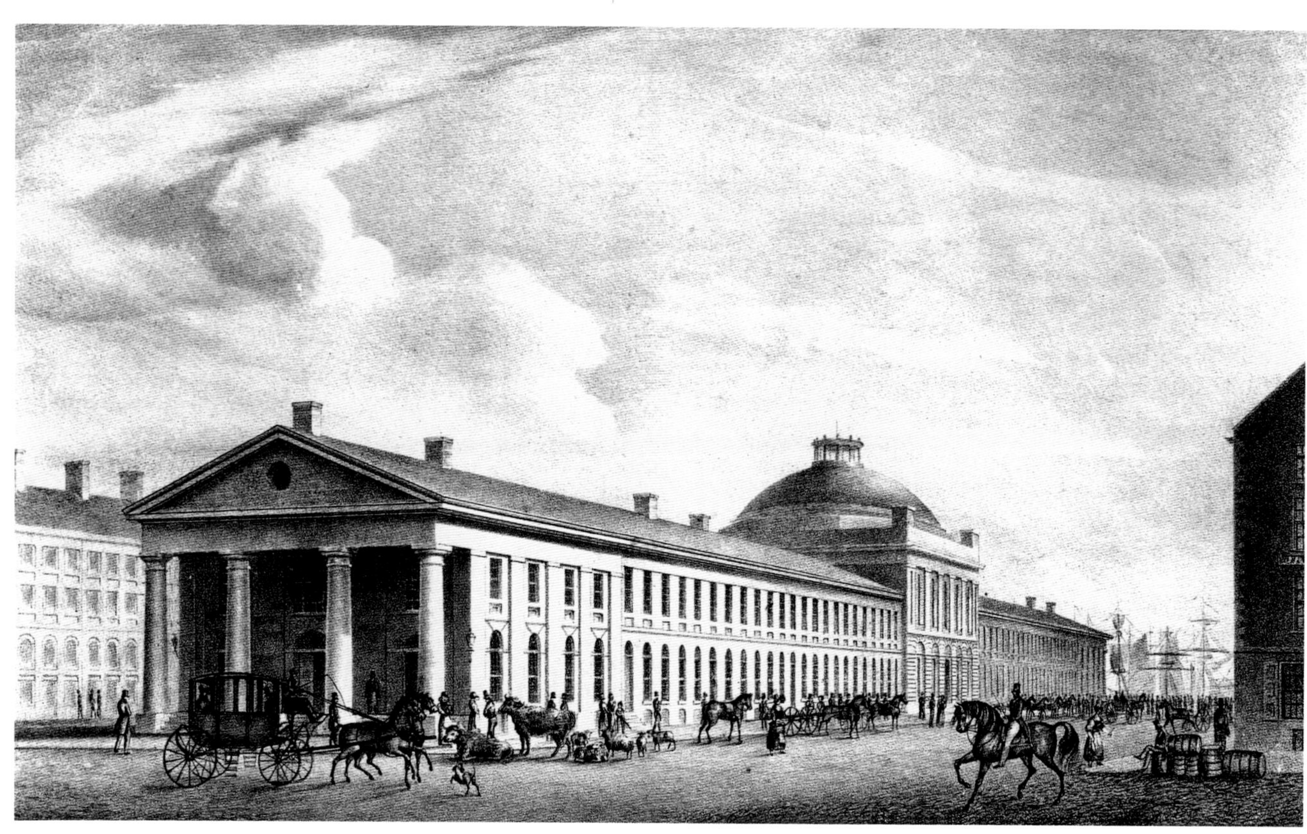

Cat. 13   Alexander Jackson Davis, *Quincy Hall Market, Boston* (1829).

class of architecture, yet produced on this side [of] the Atlantic."[21] Davis exhibited the print in 1829 at the National Academy of Design in New York, and the view was copied as an engraving many times throughout the nineteenth century. The English firm of Job and John Jackson even reproduced it on Staffordshire plates for an American market, slightly altering Davis's rendering by adding several pedestrians.[22]   C. S.

Mary Jane Derby (1807–1892).

15 **[Pickman-Derby-Brookhouse House, Salem, Massachusetts].**
Crayon lithograph on China paper backed by a secondary support of wove paper, ca. 1828. 10¾ x 12¾ in. Printed on stone l.l.: *M. J. D. del.;* l.r.: *Pendletons Litho.* [Boston].
Boston Athenæum.

This lithograph portrays the artist's childhood home in Salem, Massachusetts, at the time of her family's occupancy. Built in 1764 by the wealthy merchant, Benjamin Pickman, the house and property were sold in 1782 to Elias Hasket Derby, "the most eminent merchant that has ever been in Salem."[23] Known to his contemporaries as "King Derby," Elias Hasket Derby amassed an enormous fortune in the shipping business. The original Pickman house was apparently not regal enough for his standards, however, and he promptly hired Salem's leading architect and carpenter, Samuel McIntire, to renovate the building. McIntire first added an observation cupola topped with a gilded eagle, after which he resurfaced the entire brick front with wood boarding, built two corner Grecian style pilasters and added an ornamented portico entrance.[24] The result was a house of considerable elegance.

After the death of Elias Hasket Derby, the house was eventually occupied by his second son, John Derby, father of the artist. John Derby was not the shrewd merchant his father had been, and was content to live a quiet life of leisure surrounded by all the latest luxuries. In spite of this lack of enterprise, John Derby did make two important alterations to the building. He hired the French painter, Michele Felice Corné, to decorate the arched ceiling of the cupola with a panorama of the Derby shipping fleet, and also commissioned the coach house, seen in the left of this lithograph, after a design by Samuel McIntire.

The house remained in the Derby family for many years. Mary Jane Derby's nephew, the celebrated sculptor John Rogers, was born in the house in 1829. It was eventually sold to another wealthy Salem merchant, Robert Brookhouse In 1915, the building was demolished and a

Masonic Temple was erected on the site. The cupola was salvaged, however, and became a part of the Essex Institute's collections.   C. S.

Mary Jane Derby (1807–1892).

16 **Temple of Jupiter.**
Crayon lithograph on wove paper, 1828. 7¼ x 9¼ in. Printed on stone on image l.l.: *M. J. D. del.;* on image l.r.: *Pendletons' Lith* [Boston]. Inscribed in graphite beneath lithograph: *First attempt at Lithography — Copied — Temple Jupiter. 1828.*
Boston Athenæum purchase, 1993.

The *Temple of Jupiter*, Mary Jane Derby's "first attempt at lithography," formed part of a scrapbook she assembled that is now in the collection of the Boston Athenæum. The scrapbook contains four Pendleton lithographs signed on stone by Derby and eighteen drawings attributed to her. Two additional lithographs by James F. Colman (see above) and an unidentified artist named "Arnold" were also found in the album.

The Derby album is an excellent example of a young amateur's attempt to master the difficult art of drawing on paper and on stone. The compositions, numbered and mounted on color or white paper with black ink borders, range from the rudimentary sketch to more accomplished charcoal drawings and lithographs. Ruins, medieval and classical, were one of Derby's favorite subjects but the scrapbook also abounds with rural scenes of cottages, mills, and *chateaux*. A few of the drawings are original compositions of local scenery and appear to have been drawn *en plein air*. However, the lithographs and the majority of the drawings are clearly copied from other sources; some are annotated with a title and the phrase "copied from an engraving."

As a member of the wealthy and prominent Derby clan, Mary Jane Derby undoubtedly had access to the numerous drawing manuals published at this time. One of the more popular of these manuals was John Rubens Smith's *The Juvenile Drawing Book: Being the Rudiments of the Art, Explained in a Series of Easy Progressive Lessons*. At least seventeen editions of this manual were published in the first half of the nineteenth century. In his preface, Smith was anxious to note the participation of "young ladies" in the art of drawing: "My hitherto not appealing to the ladies in elucidating the utility of this art, is because they need not such appeal; they have long since shown their conviction of its intellectual gratification, by the numbers that strive to acquire it, and notwithstanding the difficulties they have to contend with . . . they have more proficients among them than our sex can boast of; such not

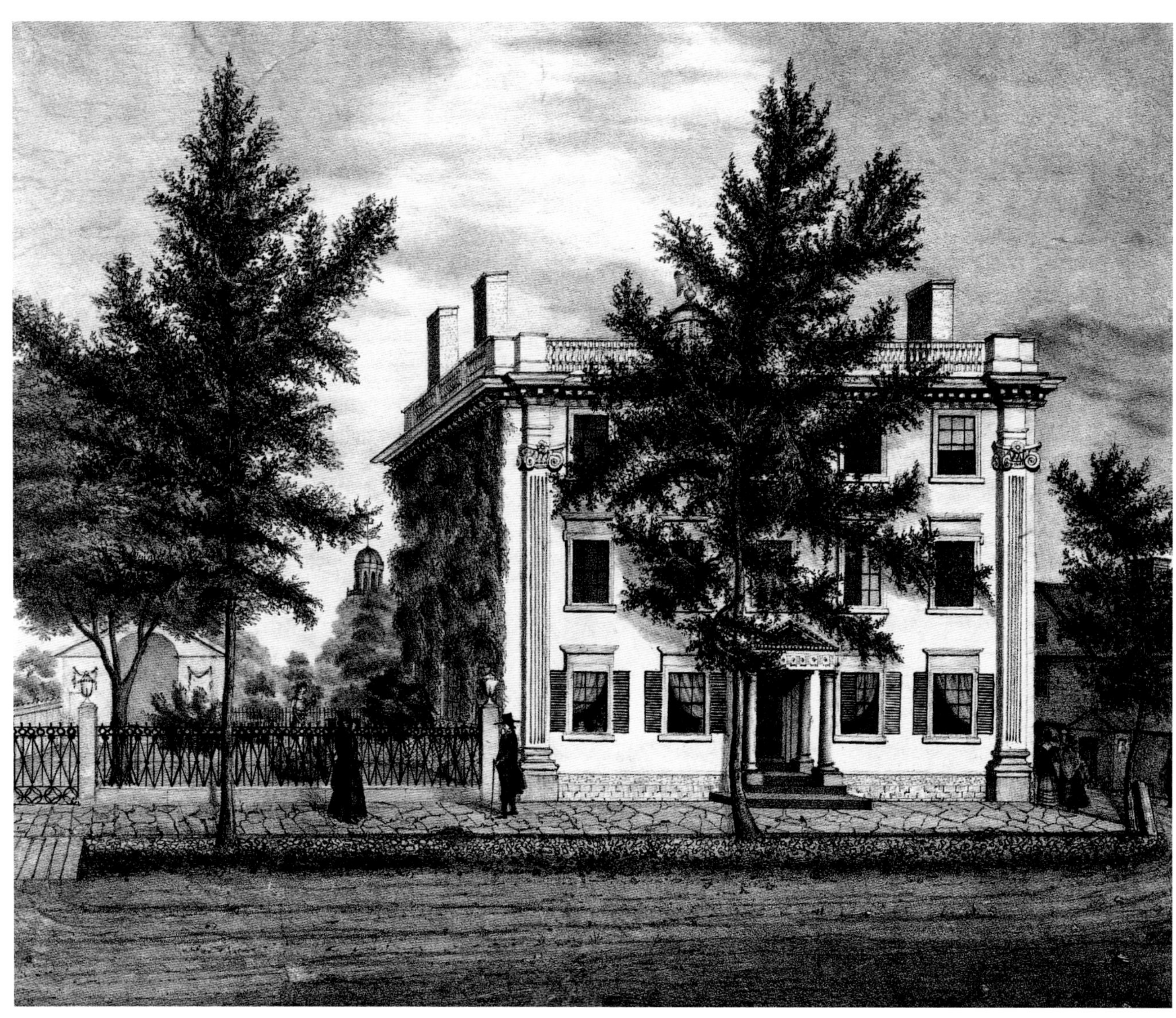

Cat. 15   Mary Jane Derby, *Pickman-Derby-Brookhouse House, Salem* (ca. 1828).

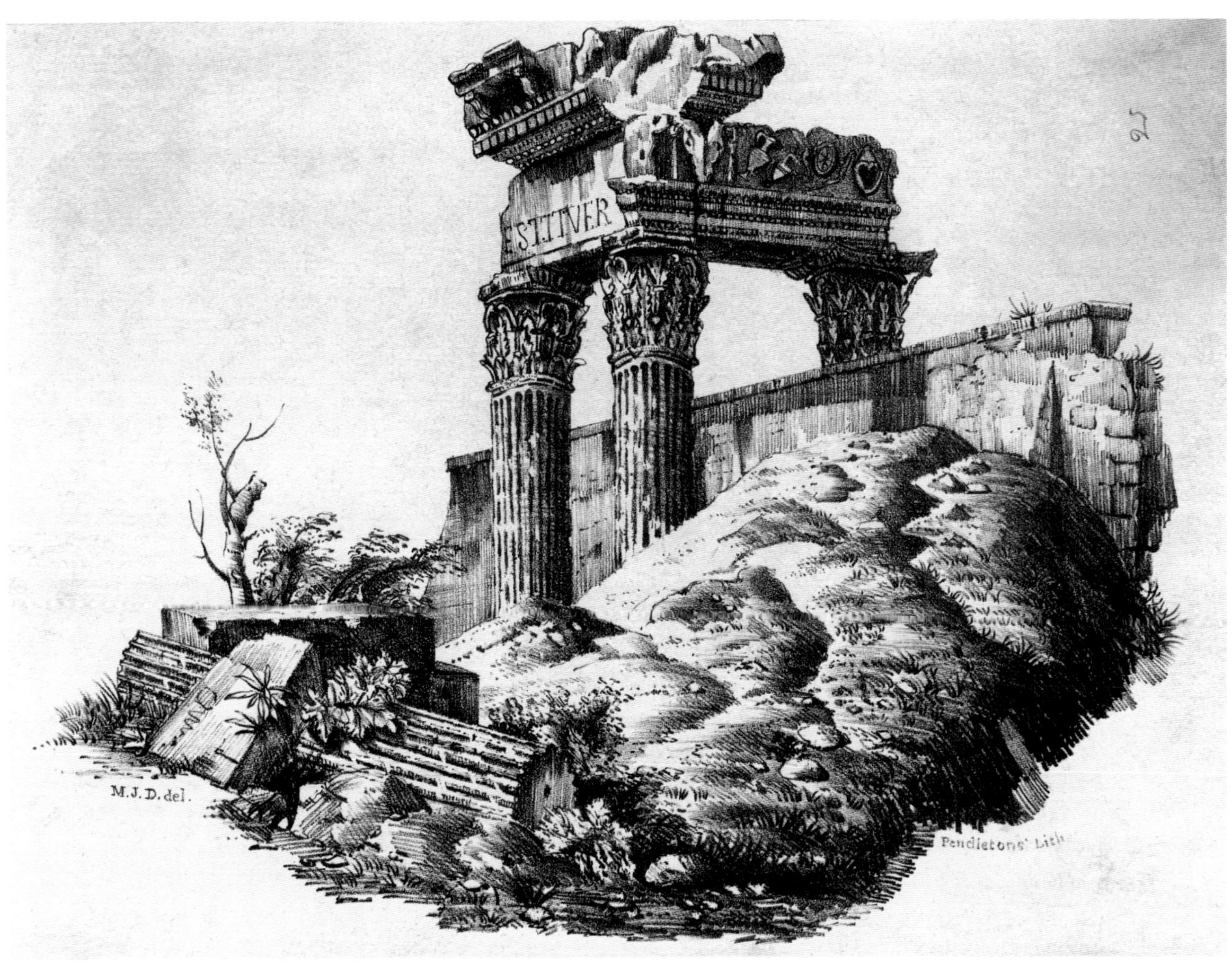

Cat. 16 Mary Jane Derby, *Temple of Jupiter* (1828).

being known, is attributable to their usually pursuing it as an accomplishment, not a profession, which, added to their natural diffidence of character, prevents their obtruding on public notice. The number of ladies to that of gentlemen, who have studied drawing, may be computed at twenty to one." c. s.

Thomas Edwards (1795–1869).

17 Lower Bridge and Factories, Dover, N. H.
Crayon lithograph with hand-coloring on wove paper, ca. 1828–1830. 11 x 14¼ in. Printed on stone l.l.: *Edwards del.;* l.r.: *Senefelder Lith. Co.*
Boston Athenæum.

Dover, New Hampshire, was a major producer of cotton textiles throughout the nineteenth century. Incorporated in 1812, the Dover Cotton Factory purchased the Lower Falls property on the Cocheco River in 1821, and over the course of the next several years erected the brick factories depicted in this lithograph. In the late 1820s and early 1830s, these buildings contained over 20,000 spindles and 700 looms. Calico printing, a major advancement in cotton manufacturing, was introduced here in 1829.

This print was probably produced in the late 1820s about the time the Cocheco Manufacturing Company bought out the Dover Cotton Manufacturing Company. Thomas Edwards' lithograph presents a scene of tranquil prosperity, however for the mill girls who worked here, these factories were neither tranquil nor monetarily rewarding. In December 1828, they held their first strike, complaining of "restrictive regulations," heavy fines imposed on tardy workers, and the prohibition against talking during the long work day.[25] c. s.

Thomas Edwards (1795–1869).

18 Rev. Enoch W. Freeman.
Crayon lithograph on tan wove paper, ca. 1828. 9¼ x 6½ in. Printed on stone l.l.: *Edwards delt.;* l.r.: *Annin & Smith … Senfr Litho Co.* [Boston].
Boston Athenæum.

In December 1828, when a notice of this lithograph appeared in *The Bower of Taste,* the Rev. Enoch W. Freeman (1798–1835) had recently been installed as pastor of Lowell's First Baptist Church. He was enormously popular with his congregation for the first four or five years of his ministry, but in 1832 the Reverend, who in this lithograph appears calm and self-confident, became the subject of notoriety when he began a two-year courtship of his cousin. Hannah Hanson was considered by many members of the First Baptist Church to be a loose

woman and an improper choice for a minister's wife. She was divorced and was said to be on intimate terms with, if not engaged to, a Boston gentleman by the name of George T. Kinney. A scandal erupted and church committees were formed to look into their courtship. Their report concluded that, although Rev. Freeman and Hannah Hanson had shown a certain "carelessness" in their conduct, "there was no substantial reason to implicate [their] moral character."[26] Within weeks of the release of this report, Rev. Freeman married Hannah Hanson on September 23, 1834.

But rumors regarding Mrs. Freeman's improprieties continued to circulate in Lowell. Her former suitor from Boston, George T. Kinney, visited the Freeman's house frequently. Indeed, he was there on September 20, 1835, when the Rev. Freeman suddenly became violently ill. He complained of abdominal pains and vomited frequently. On September 22, 1835, at the age of thirty-seven, the Rev. Freeman died, just one day short of his first wedding anniversary. The cause of death was officially reported as "Chlorea Morbus,"[27] but some of Lowell's citizens weren't so sure. Suspicions about Mrs. Freeman's possible role in the death of her husband abounded.[28]

The resulting atmosphere was disagreeable enough to force Mrs. Freeman to move to Boston, where, within fourteen months of Rev. Freeman's death, she married George T. Kinney. Four years later, Mr. Kinney suffered the same unfortunate fate as Rev. Freeman. The symptoms were identical, and this time the widow was brought to trial under accusations of poisoning her husband. A team of doctors, including Dr. Jacob Bigelow and Dr. James Jackson, determined that Kinney had died of arsenic poisoning.[29] A jury refused to convict her, however, and she quickly published a book about her experiences in an attempt to clear her name, *A Review of the Principal Events of the Last Ten Years in the Life of Mrs. Hannah Kinney.* Many Lowell citizens, and especially members of the First Baptist Church, were not convinced of her innocence, and questions resurfaced about the death of Reverend Freeman. His body was exhumed and, although four years had passed, there were no signs of decay — a clear indication of arsenic poisoning. c. s.

Eliza Goodridge (1798–1882).

19 Round Hill, Northampton.
Crayon lithograph on wove paper, ca, 1827. 8½ x 12 in. Printed on stone l.l.: *Miss. E. Goodridge pinxt. et del.;* l.r.: *Pendleton's Lithographers Boston.*
Boston Athenæum purchase, 1994.

Round Hill School was established in 1823 by George Bancroft and Joseph Green Cogswell. Both men were

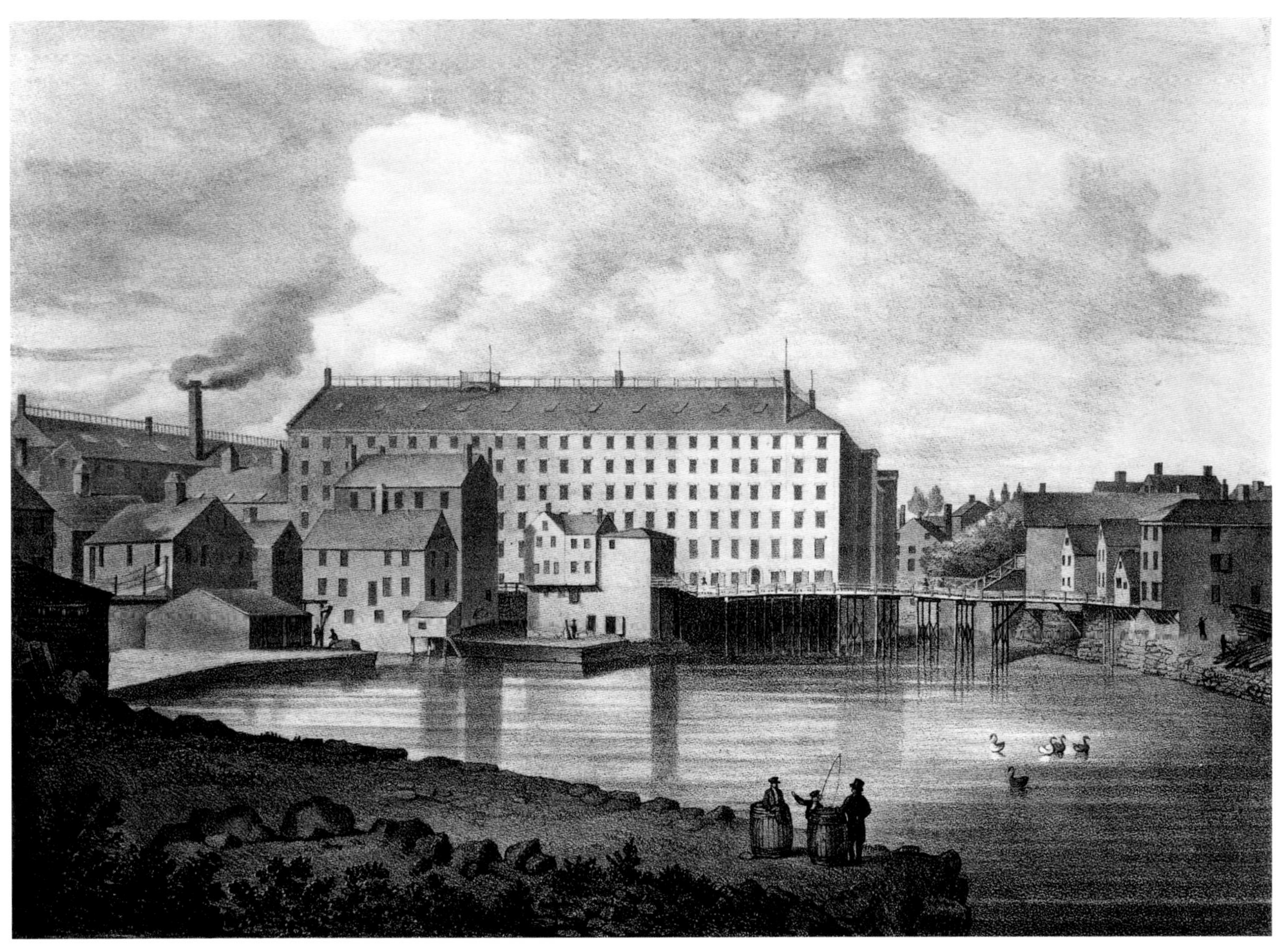

Cat. 17   Thomas Edwards, *Lower Bridge and Factories, Dover, N. H.* (ca. 1828–1830).

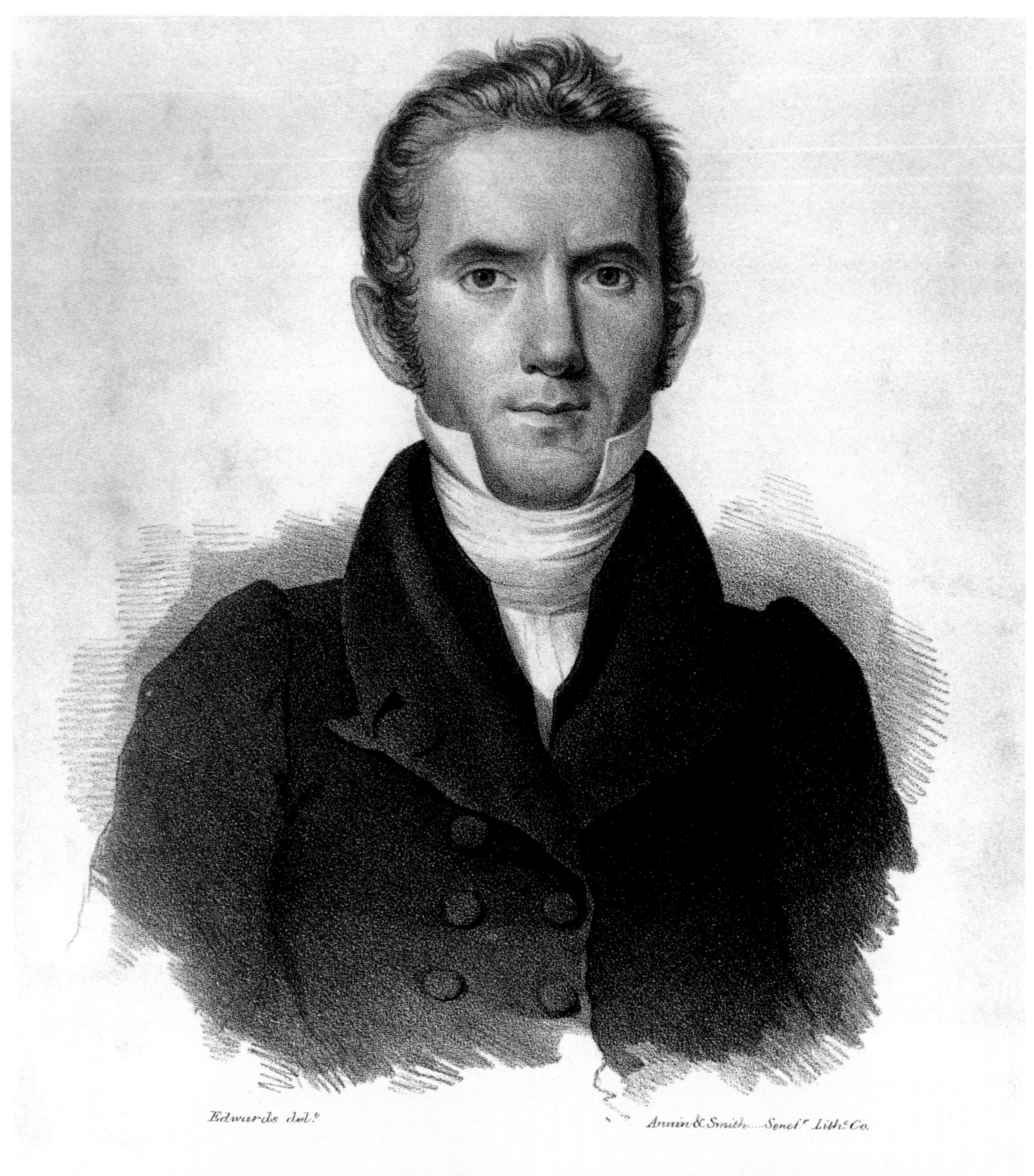

Cat. 18 Thomas Edwards, *Rev. Enoch W. Freeman* (ca. 1828).

44

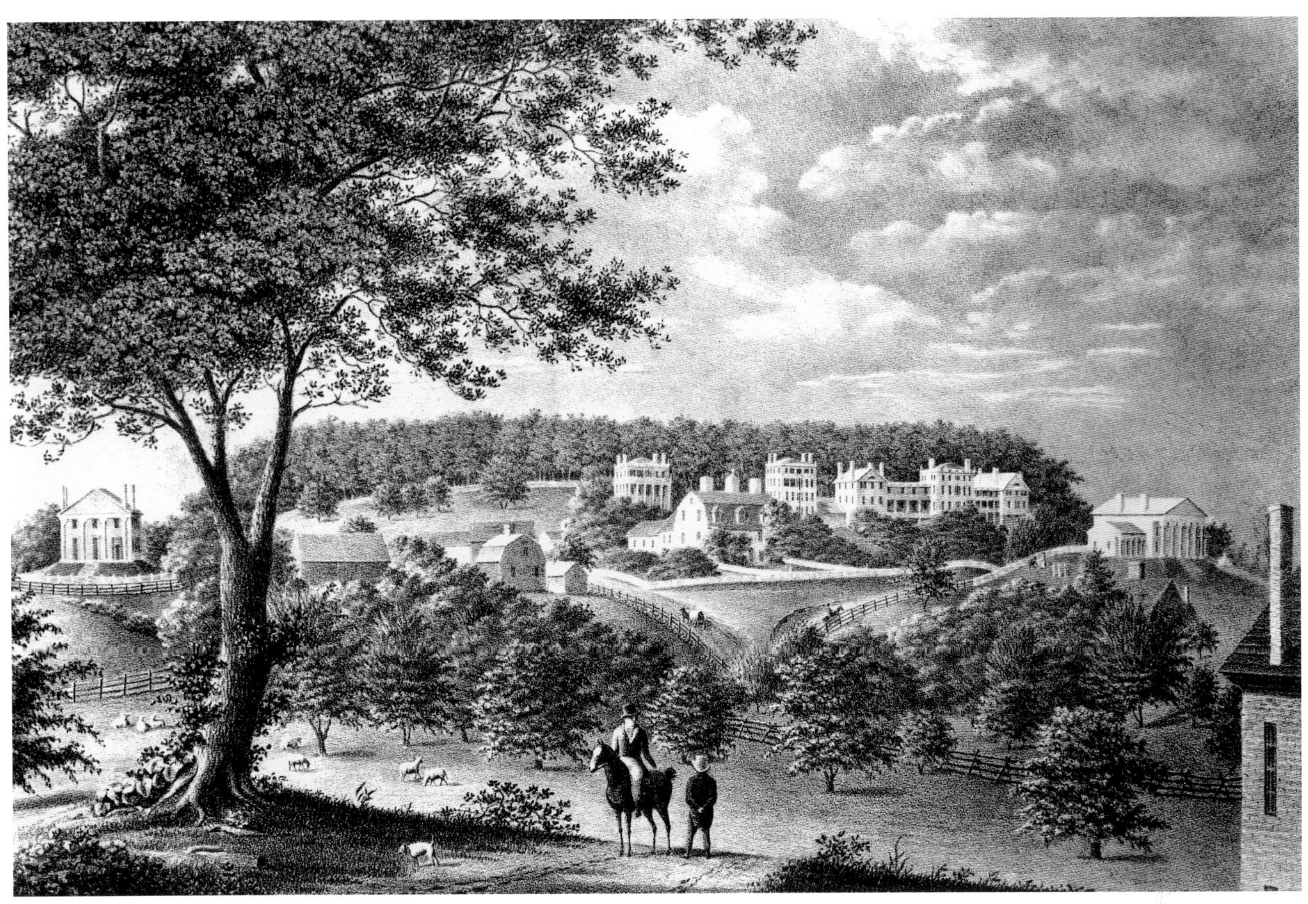

Cat. 19   Eliza Goodridge, *Round Hill, Northampton* (ca. 1827).

Harvard graduates and had studied in Europe where they were deeply influenced by the German and French pedagogical reforms. Their attempts at educational reforms having been frustrated while tutoring at Harvard, they decided to establish their own experimental preparatory school, based on the concept of German *gymnasia*. The site they chose, near the village of Northampton, Massachusetts, was picked for its "quiet shades, its healthy atmosphere, its beautiful scenery."[30] A prospectus of the school stated that the location united "salubrity and beauty . . . [to] an eminent degree."[31]

As with so many patriots of the early Republic, Cogswell and Bancroft were intensely idealistic, eager to elevate the intellectual status of the new democracy. "We think [the school] the surest way of doing something to improve the condition of our county and to promote the cause of virtue and learning."[32] Round Hill provided its students with rigorous intellectual training, emphasizing English, natural history and modern languages. Gymnastics and strenuous physical exercise were seen as means to instill moral purity in their pupils.

From the outset the school was highly controversial. Reforms such as the elimination of reward and punishment were considered extremely radical. Its notoriety, however, only increased its popularity, and the school grew rapidly from 25 students in 1823 to 135 in 1827. Although the school's founders emphasized the moral virtues of integrating rich and poor students, the enrollment list — including names such as Amory, Appleton, Howe, Lawrence, Shaw, and Ward — reads like a "who's who" of prominent New England families.

In spite of its success, the school eventually ran into debt and closed in the spring of 1834; the school's founders went on to pursue their own intellectual interests. Cogswell became the first librarian of the famed Astor Library in New York, and Bancroft distinguished himself as a nationally known diplomat and historian.   C. S.

Eliza Goodridge (1798–1882).
20   A View of Round Hill, Northampton, Mass.
Gray wash on wove paper, ca. 1827. 7½ x 11¼ in.
Boston Athenæum purchase, 1994.

This preparatory drawing for the lithograph above, was one of seven renderings of Round Hill, Northampton, by the artist Eliza Goodridge. Overlooking the lush Connecticut River Valley, Round Hill was named for its shape and renowned for its singular beauty. The Hill was the site of two outstanding examples of early Greek Revival architecture. On the far right of this drawing is the colonnaded mansion of Joseph Bower. Designed in

1825 by the celebrated architect Ithiel Town (1784–1844), the dwelling was considered so spectacular that an engraving of it was published in various editions of J. H. Hinton's popular *History and Topography of the United States*. A year later, Town designed the less ostentatious Greek Revival house on the far left for a gentleman named Charles Dewey. The building later became part of Smith College in 1871.[33]

The cluster of stately buildings in the center belonged to the prestigious Round Hill School (see above). The school had originally consisted of three Federal style homes built by the Shepherd family in the first decade of the nineteenth century. To accommodate the growing number of students, the school was enlarged in 1827 by adding wings and an ell. There has been some speculation that these additions were also designed by Ithiel Town. After the school closed in 1834, the buildings were eventually sold to the Round Hill Water Cure Retreat Company for $15,000. In 1867, the Clarke School for the Deaf took over the buildings and part of the property.[34]   C. S.

James Herring (1794–1867).
21   [Kittens].
Crayon lithograph with hand coloring on wove paper, ca. 1829. 10¾ x 14¾ in. Printed on stone l.l.: *Drawn by I. Herring;* l.c.: *Published by M. Bancroft, 403 Broadway;* l.r.: *Printed at P. Maverick's Lithy.*
American Antiquarian Society; gift of Benjamin Tighe, 1949.

22   [Puppies].
Crayon lithograph with hand coloring on wove paper, ca. 1829. 9½ x 15 in. Printed on stone l.l.: *Drawn by I. Herring;* l.r.: *Printed by P. Maverick.*
American Antiquarian Society; gift of Benjamin Tighe, 1949.

Puppies and *Kittens*, drawn on stone by James Herring, are typical of inexpensive prints designed to be framed. Herring was a multi-talented individual, working as a portrait painter, book publisher, library proprietor, distiller, and school teacher. Beginning in 1822, he had a studio in New York. The two lithographs were printed by Peter Maverick, whose family was active in all aspects of the visual arts in New York. His four daughters were all taught the basics of lithography, and Herring himself may have gone to the Maverick shop to experiment with the new medium.

Diminutive reproductions of these two prints appeared on the hat and the skirt of the *Connoisseur*, printed by Senefelder in Boston about 1830. The firm issued other prints of animals, including quails, rabbits, dogs, monkeys, woodcocks, and snipes, the titles of some of these known only through the probate records of Peter Maverick's estate.[35]   G. B.

David Claypoole Johnston (1798–1865).

23 A Brief Ejectment. Xenophon's Retreat *Out* of the Enemy's Country.
Crayon lithograph on wove paper, 1827. 7½ x 9 in. American Antiquarian Society.

24 "The Crack'd Joke." A Late Student.
Crayon lithograph on wove paper, 1827. 9¼ x 9¼ in. American Antiquarian Society.

In October 1827, politician John Agg sent a sketch of *"The Crack'd Joke"* from Washington to Daniel Webster in Boston. Webster in turn commissioned David Claypoole Johnston to produce a satirical print showing the editor of the *United States Telegraph*, Duff Green (1791–1875), teaching the Devil to lie. Although Duff Green is the target of the cartoon, his co-editor, Russell Jarvis, was cited in the sketch as "an able assistant." Jarvis was furious when he learned of the print and, in a fit of anger, went to the Pendleton shop where he apparently damaged the lithographic stone with the cartoon on it. After the scuffle, the Pendleton brothers forced him off their premises — the scene that is shown in *A Brief Ejectment.*

Rarely has there been so much information recorded about a political print. John Agg only wanted one hundred copies of the print for distribution in Washington, a rather small edition. The incident received a great deal of coverage in the Boston newspapers, particularly since Jarvis accused Senator Webster of playing a major part in the scheme to slander him.[36] Pictorial political satire was not yet a common phenomenon; in later years politicians became somewhat oblivious to it.   G. B.

David Claypoole Johnston (1798–1865).

25 Gymnastics.
Crayon lithograph on wove paper, ca. 1828. 8 x 10½ in. Printed on stone l.l.: *D. C. Johnston delt.;* l.r.: *Lith. of Pendleton* [Boston].
Boston Athenæum.

The popularity of gymnastics in early nineteenth-century Europe was largely due to the efforts of Franz Ludwig Jahn (1778–1852), who established the first major gymnasium in Berlin. Known as the "Father of Gymnastics," Jahn's influential *Treatise on Gymnastics*

(1816) extolled the virtues of physical exercise and led to the creation of gymnasiums all over Europe. In the United States, his book was translated in 1828 by Charles Beck, a young gymnastics instructor at Round Hill School (see above). This English edition of the *Treatise* was widely circulated and helped to create an enormous enthusiasm for gymnastics both in Boston and throughout the Republic.

American promoters of gymnastics emphasized not only the physical benefits to be gained, but also the contributions gymnastics could make to a fledging democracy. In his preface to the translation of the *Treatise*, Beck suggested that gymnasiums would benefit a young democracy by providing a place where "all the different classes of the people" could meet.[37] Indeed, when a Boston gymnasium was formed on Jahnian principles, the public was reminded that "enlightened nations" such as "Sparta had Gymnasia . . . What stronger argument in favour of exercises can be addressed to a republican community, whose integrity and strength depend so directly on the united energies of the citizens which compose it?"[38]

The Boston Gymnasium was "intended . . . to counteract the enervating influence which refinement and luxury must exert on the constitution."[39] In the lithograph entitled *Gymnastics*, the exercisers are not constrained by any degree of refinement. True to his satirical nature, D. C. Johnston evinced considerable skepticism about the new fad. In addition to the clumsy antics of the participants, Johnston has added a building with signs reading "Amputating Room," "Ready Made Coffins," and "Artificial Corns for Sale."   C. S.

David Claypoole Johnston (1798–1865).

26 Mr. E. Forrest as Metamora. In Mr. Stone's New Prize Tragedy.
Crayon lithograph with scratching out on India paper, ca. 1830. 11¼ x 8 in. Printed on stone l.l.: *Drawn on stone by D. C. Johnston;* l.r.: *Lith. of Pendleton. Boston.*
American Antiquarian Society; gift of Charles Henry Taylor.

David Claypoole Johnston's interest in theatrical portraits was a natural outgrowth of his career as an actor on the Philadelphia stage in the early 1820s. Most of his portraits concentrate on costume and character, but in *Metamora*, his most fully developed theatrical portrait, the setting is as elaborate as the costume. Over a period of fifteen years, Johnston engraved or lithographed nearly thirty prints in this genre.

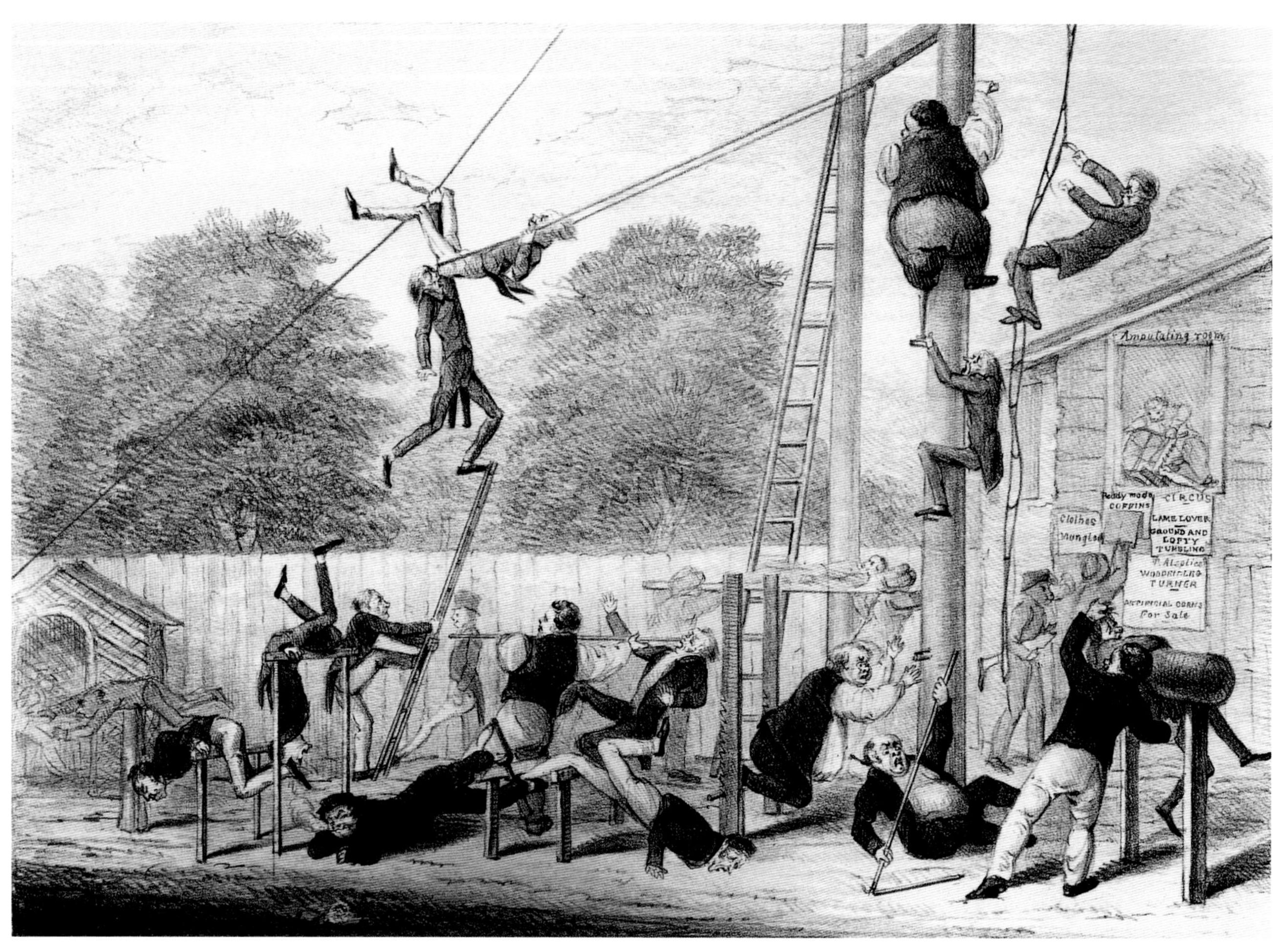

Cat. 25   David Claypoole Johnston, *Gymnastics* (ca. 1828).

48

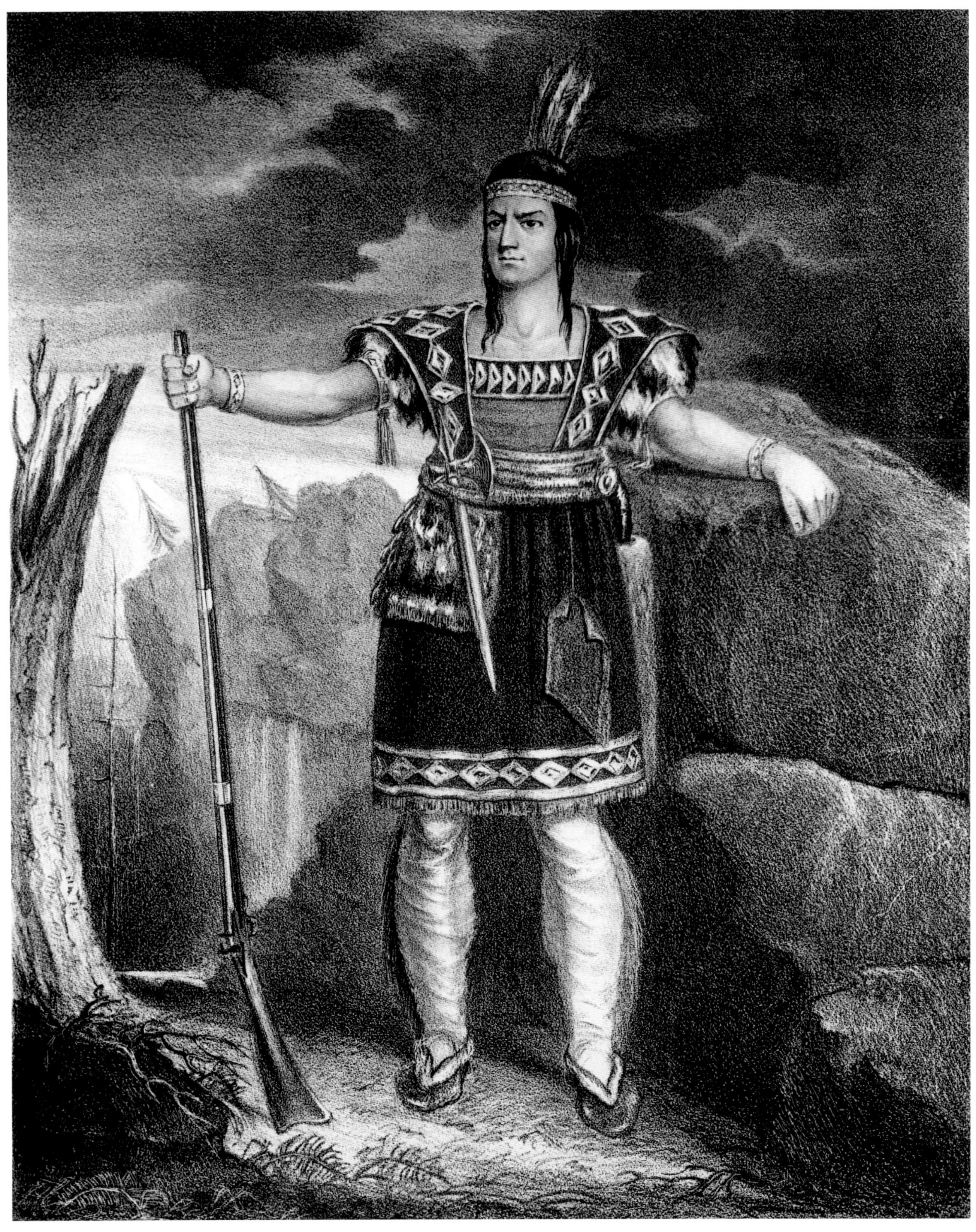

Cat. 26　David Claypoole Johnston, *Mr. E. Forrest as Metamora* (ca. 1830).

Edwin Forrest (1806–1872), then just twenty-three years old, was one of America's foremost actors. Among his other activities, he sponsored competitions to foster the writing of plays on American subjects. John August Stone, the author of *Metamora, or The Last of the Wampanoags*, won the first of these competitions.[40] The play was produced in Boston on May 17, 1830.   G. B.

David Claypoole Johnston (1798–1865).

27   Quincy Rail-Way.
Crayon lithograph on wove paper, ca. 1826. 7 x 12 in. Inscribed on stone on image: *D C J;* Printed on stone l.l.: *Lith. of Pendleton;* l.r.: *Sold by A. J. Allen No 72 State street;* l.c.: *Rail-way Wheels.*
Boston Athenæum.

The town of Quincy was renowned for its granite quarries. When the Bunker Hill Monument Association was formed, its architect, Solomon Willard (1783–1861), and its master builder, Gridley Bryant (1789–1867), were determined to use the beautiful and high quality granite from Quincy, and with funds provided by Dr. John C. Warren, Bryant purchased a quarry in Quincy for the sole purpose of providing granite for the proposed Monument. The quarry was over three miles from Charlestown, and to solve the problem of transporting large quantities of heavy granite, Bryant, an irrepressible inventor, decided to design a railroad. The enterprise was funded by the wealthy Boston merchant Thomas Handasyd Perkins.

The Quincy Railroad had the distinction of being the first railroad in America, and consisted of three carts drawn by a horse. A Boston newspaper proudly pointed out that "this original railroad has been effected by native enterprize [*sic*] and skill, without the aid of transatlantic surveys or information."[41] In this lithograph the driver is shown gleefully pointing to three struggling horses or oxen and a single cart in the background, a form of transportation Bryant's railroad would soon replace. In the foreground is a diagram of Bryant's railway wheel. The wheels were unusually high, measuring 6½ feet in diameter, and were considered highly innovative at the time.

The railroad's first trip on October 7, 1826, generated a great deal of excitement. Newspaper accounts were extensive, the *Columbian Centinel* of October 11, 1826, noting that "three wagons, each weighing five tons and filled with sixteen tons of granite, were moved with ease by a single horse." The railroad terminated at the Neponset Bridge, where the granite was removed and taken by boats to Charlestown for use in the Bunker Hill monument.

Bryant resisted the use of steam power, and the railroad operated in much the same manner for several

50

decades. It was used to convey granite for the construction of other Boston buildings such as the Tremont House and the Custom House. Bryant did not patent his invention and received no monetary rewards for his efforts; he died in poverty in 1867. Three years later, the Quincy Railway was purchased by the Old Colony Railroad and the horses were eventually replaced by steam power.[42]   C. S.

James Kidder (1793–1837).

28   Boston Common.
Crayon lithograph, 1829. 11½ x 15¾ in. Printed on stone beneath image l.l.: *Drawn by James Kidder;* l.c.: *Published by Abel Bowen.;* l.r.: *Senefelder Litho Co.*
Boston Athenæum; gift of Nathaniel Kidder, 1935.

The publication of this lithograph received the following review in the May 23, 1829, edition of Boston's *Columbian Centinel:*

We have before us a lively view of the Common lithographed by Senefelder, from a drawing by Kidder. The State House and buildings on Beacon and Park streets, together with the Malls, and some edifices in the background appear in beautiful perspective. We miss, however, the elegant blocks on each side of the Hancock Mansion, and presume the drawing was done before they were constructed. We should also have been better pleased if the view had extended a little farther towards the right, so as to have admitted the lofty tower of Park-street Church. With these exceptions, the lithograph presents one of the finest views of this elegant scene that we have met. The mall fences, the intersecting paths, and the trees scattered about, are in just proportion: the people promenading, and the dogs sporting about, and the cows grazing at leisure, appear like nature herself. We should also have liked to have seen the boys playing ball: we presume however, that it was sketched at a moment when the young urchins were at their books in school. On the whole, it is well executed, and is worthy of a gilt frame.   C. S.

James Kidder (1793–1837).

29   Crown & Eagle Mills, Uxbridge, Mass.
Crayon lithograph with hand-coloring on wove paper, ca. 1829. 14 x 16¼ in. Printed on stone l.l.: *James Kidder del.;* l.r.: *Senefelder Litho. Co.* [Boston].
Boston Athenæum.

North Uxbridge, Massachusetts, was a manufacturing town thirty-eight miles southwest of Boston, strategically located on the turnpike between Boston and Hartford. The Crown & Eagle Mills were the largest cotton-mills in

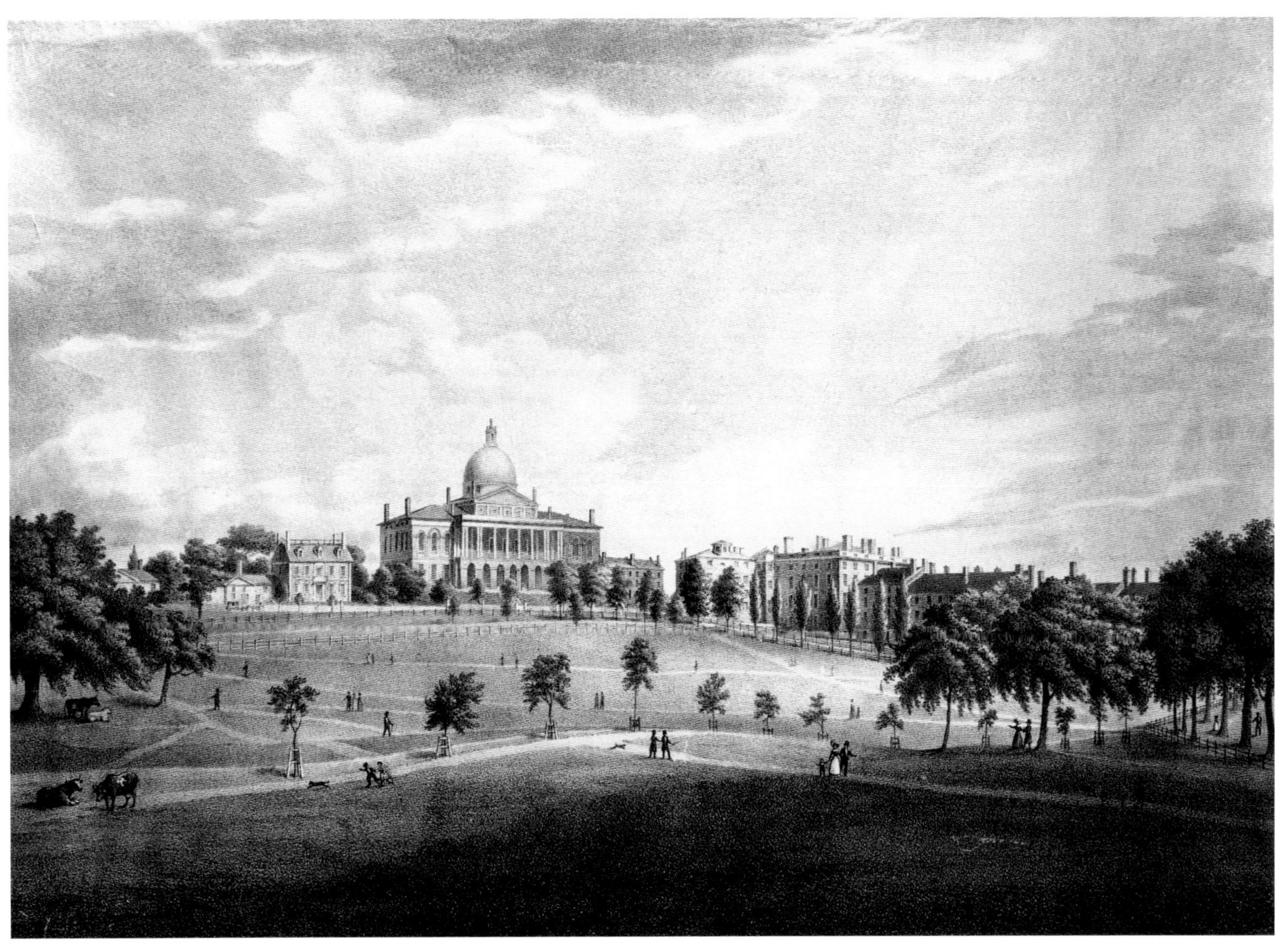

Cat. 28 James Kidder, *Boston Common* (1829).

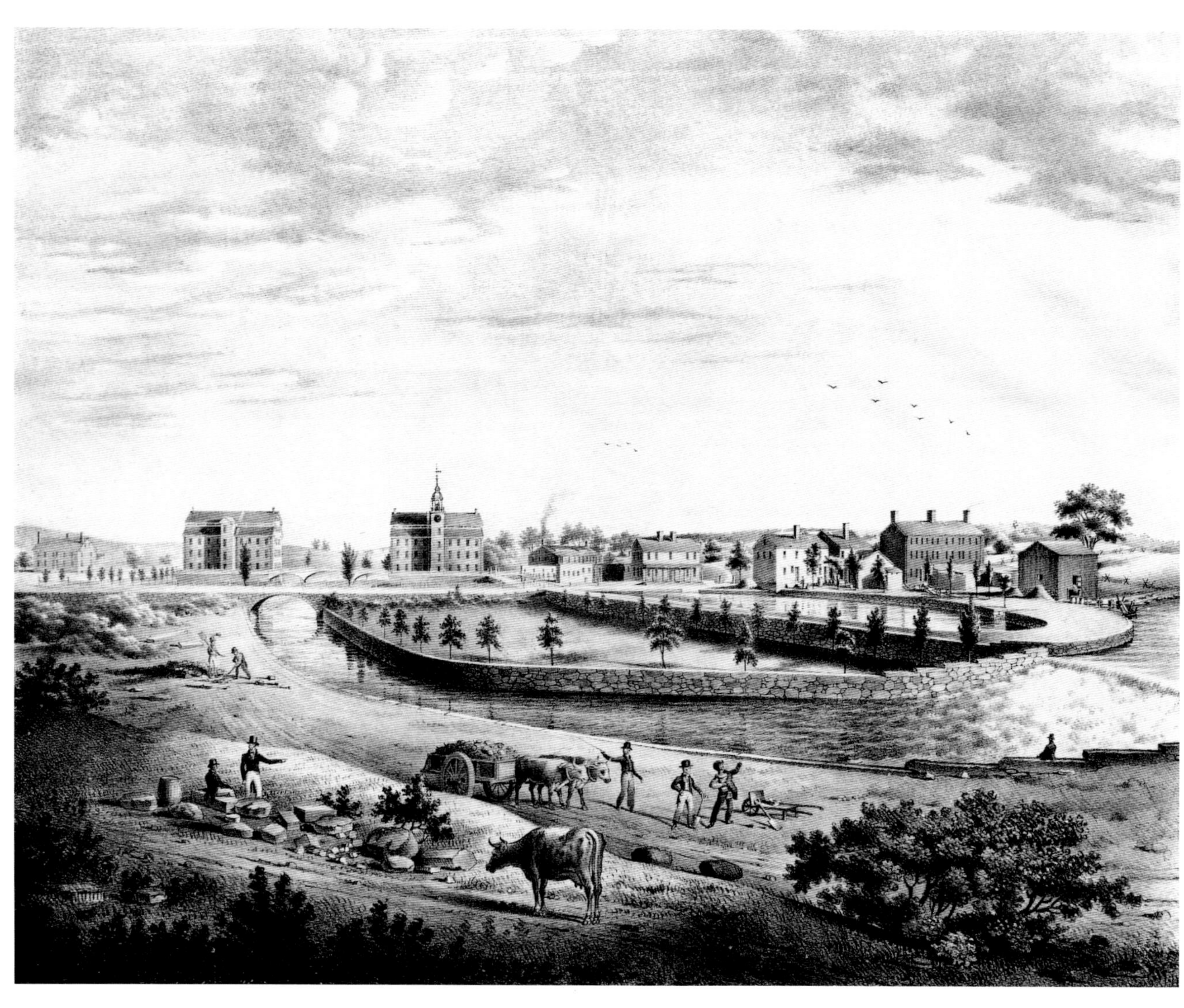

Cat. 29   James Kidder, *Crown & Eagle Mills, Uxbridge, Mass.* (ca. 1829).

Uxbridge. In 1817, Roger Rogerson, a friend of the mill pioneer Samuel Slater, purchased a small mill on the site of the Mumford River, where he raised a dam and in 1823 built a granite stone mill which he called the "Crown." In 1827 he built a "sister" mill just to the east. Known as the "Eagle" mill, it was identical to the "Crown" except that it lacked a bell cupola. Rogerson named his mills to represent England, his mother country, and the United States, to which he had immigrated. Both mills made use of clerestory monitors — a row of windows along the roof — to increase the amount of interior light, and these can be seen clearly in the two mills in this lithograph.

Rogerson attempted to beautify the site and landscaped the grounds with trees and artificial ponds. The brick buildings on the right of this lithograph were accommodations for the workers and their families. The community eventually became known as "Rogerson's Village," and received praise for its "perfection." Rogerson failed financially in 1837; the property was taken over by his creditors and became known as the Uxbridge Cotton Mills.[43]   C. S.

James Kidder (1793–1837).

30   View of the Quincy Temple.
Crayon lithograph on wove paper, ca. 1828–1829. 11¾ x 13½ in. Printed on stone l.l.: *Drawn on stone by J. Kidder.;* l.r.: *Annin & Smith…Senefelder Litho. Co.* [Boston].
Boston Athenæum.

In 1822, former President John Adams donated several granite quarries to his hometown of Quincy, Massachusetts, with the provision that the stones be used to erect a new meeting house for the First Parish Church, the construction of which did not begin until after his death. In September of 1826, then President John Quincy Adams requested that "a plain and modest monument . . . divested of all ostentation" be erected to his father's memory.[44] He stipulated that the monument be a part of the new Temple of the First Parish Church.

At the urging of Boston Mayor Josiah Quincy, himself a former citizen of Quincy, the church committee hired architect Alexander Parris, who had just completed the much admired Quincy Market in Boston (see above). His Doric style temple was designed in consultation with President John Quincy Adams, who impressed Parris with his knowledge of European architecture. The church committee was adamant that only the very exquisite "blue" granite from Adams' quarries be used. Each of the four front columns were made from one stone, and it took eighty oxen and dozens of men to transport the monolithic columns from the quarry to the site of the new Temple, where a special "hoisting apparatus" was used to raise them. They stood over twenty-two feet tall and were over four feet in diameter.

The church was dedicated on November 12, 1828. Although James Kidder titled his lithograph *Quincy Temple*, the church was universally known as the Stone Temple. Two granite chambers had been built under the portico for the remains of John Adams and his wife; later John Quincy Adams and his wife would also be buried there. Inside the Temple, on either side of the pulpit, stood two marble tablets with busts of the two presidents, the bust of John Adams by Horatio Greenough, and that of John Quincy Adams by Hiram Powers.   C. S.

William B. Lucas (fl. 1828–1833).

31   The Orphan.
Crayon lithograph with hand coloring on wove paper, ca. 1829. 7¾ x 5½ in. Printed on stone l.l.: *On Stone by W. B. Lucas;* l.r.: *Kennedy & Lucas Lithography* [Philadelphia].
American Antiquarian Society.

William B. Lucas established the first lithographic firm in Philadelphia in 1828. By December of that year he was joined in his business by David Kennedy, who was, like Lucas, a gilder of mirror and picture frames. The firm published several architectural views, portraits, and genre prints such as *The Orphan*, which was drawn on stone by Lucas and may reproduce a painting of the same subject. The desolate nature of the graveyard is emphasized by the broken fence, and the dead branches of the tree and the enormous cavity in its trunk. The church spire holds out the possibility of consolation, while the evergreen bough on the grave symbolizes hope. Kennedy and Lucas would have sold their own prints in their shop as well as prints imported from Europe.   G. B.

Gherlando Marsiglia (1792–1850).

32   Napoleon au Bivouac.
Crayon lithograph with hand coloring on wove paper, ca. 1830. 16¼ x 11¼ in. Printed on stone l.l.: *On Stone by G. Marsiglia;* l.r.: *Lithography of Imbert* [New York City].
American Antiquarian Society.

Napoleon was a popular figure in America, and numerous prints of him were published in the 1820s and 1830s. Jacques Louis David's painting of the coronation of Napoleon, *Le Sacre,* for example, was exhibited in New

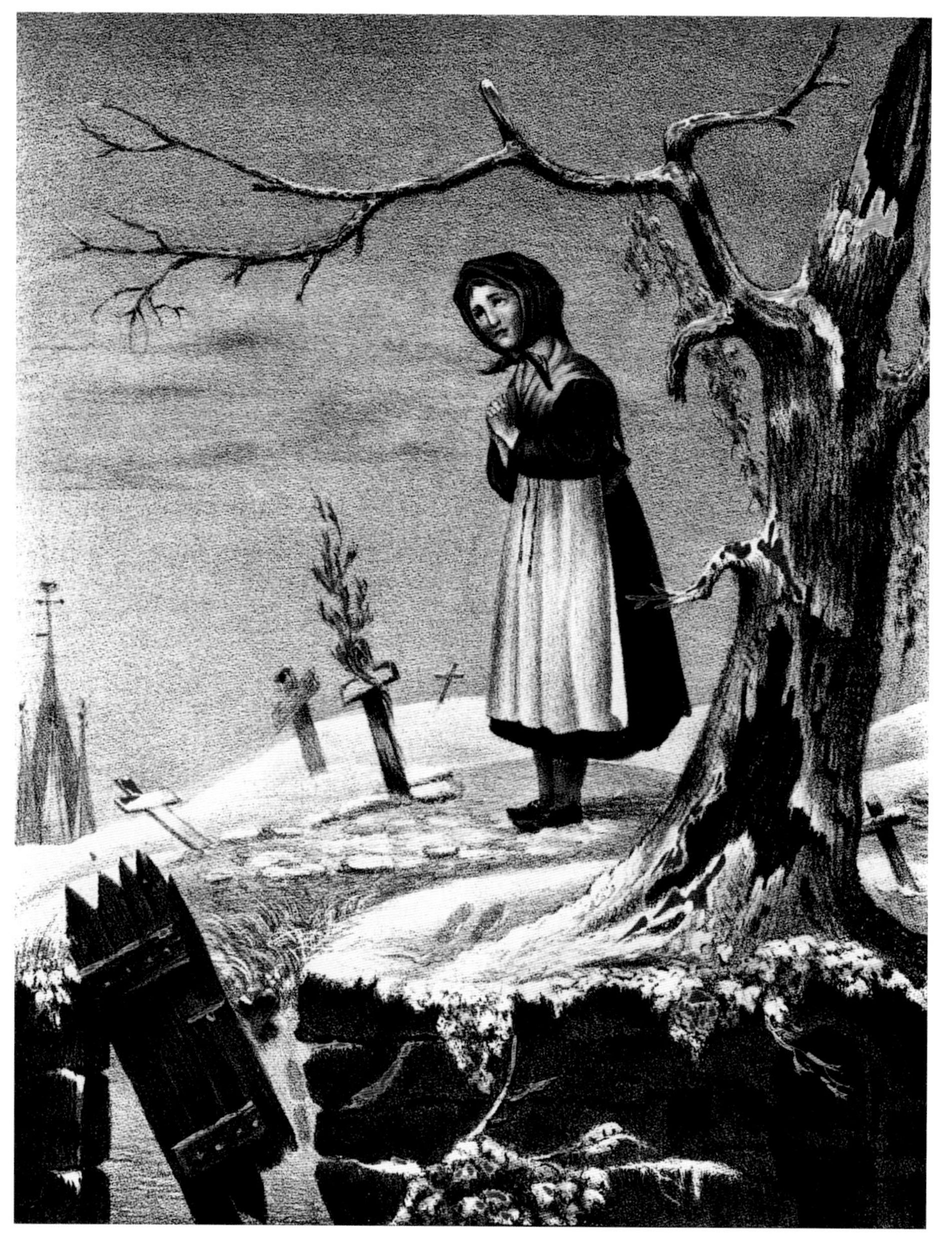

Cat. 31   William B. Lucas, *The Orphan* (ca. 1829).

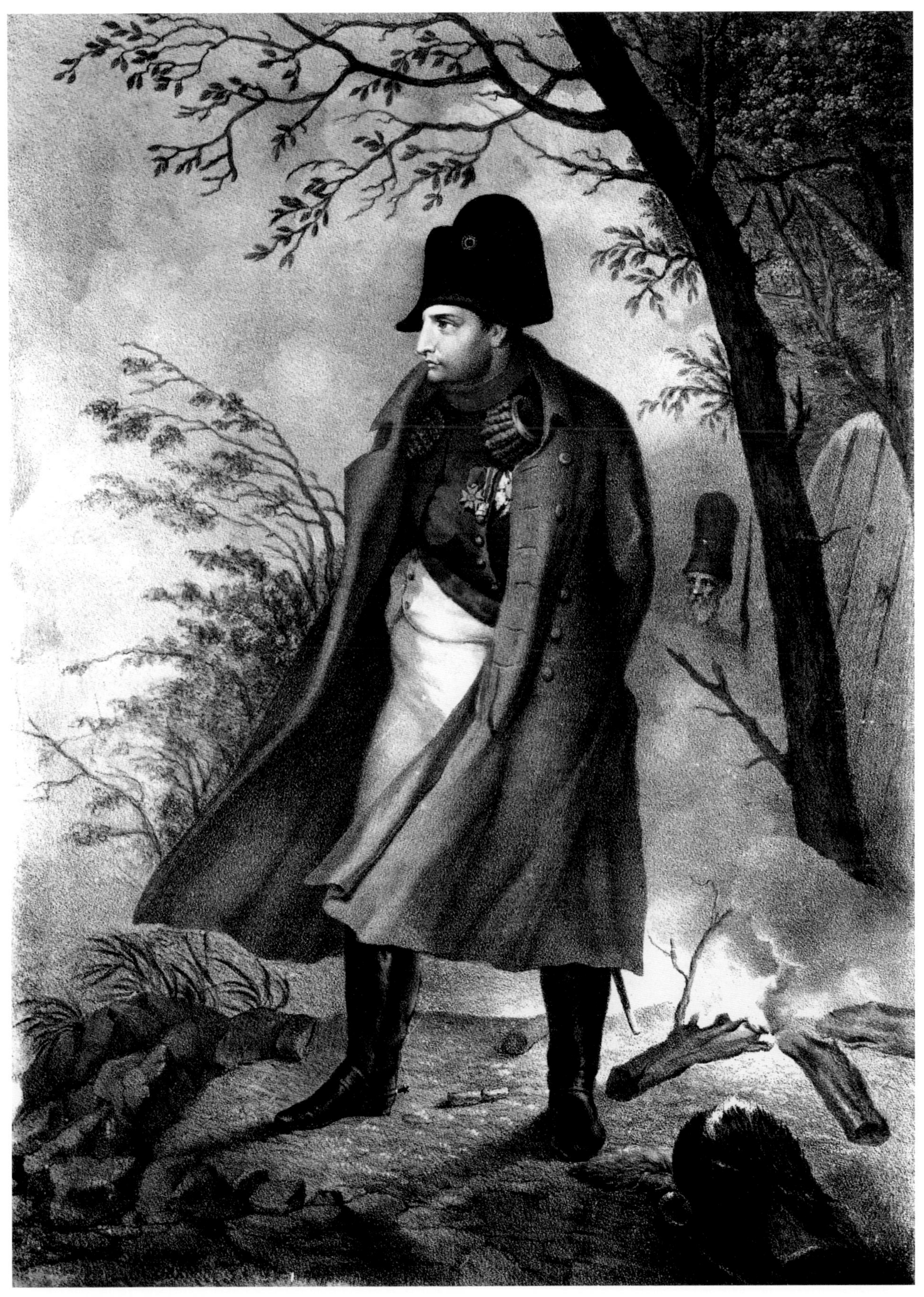

Cat. 32   Gherlando Marsiglia, *Napoleon au Bivouac* (ca. 1830).

York in 1826. *Napoleon au Bivouac* was drawn on stone by
Gherlando Marsiglia, an Italian portrait and landscape
artist, who came to New York in 1817. It is similar in style
to the work of the French lithographer Denis-Auguste-
Marie Raffet (1804–1860) and his teachers Baron Antoine-
Jean Gros (1771–1835) and the military artist Nicolas-
Toussaint Charlet (1792–1845). Between 1826 and 1828,
Raffet published twenty-four lithographic plates in an
album entitled *Histoire de Napoléon*. The elongated hel-
met of the soldier in the rear of this lithograph suggests
that the opposition army was of Russian origin.   G. B.

Nicolas-Eustache Maurin (1799–1850).

**33   George Washington, First President of the United
States.**
Crayon lithograph on India paper, 1825–1828. 13½ x
9¾ in. Printed on stone l.r.: *Entered according to the
Act of Congress.*
American Antiquarian Society; gift of Charles Henry
Taylor.

**34   John Adams, Second President of the United
States.**
Crayon lithograph on wove paper, 1825–1828. 13¾ x
9¾ in. Printed on stone l.c.: *From the Original Series
painted by Stuart. for the Messrs. Doggett of Boston. /
Entered according to the Act of Congress.*
American Antiquarian Society; gift of Charles Henry
Taylor.

**35   Thomas Jefferson, Third President of the United
States.**
Crayon lithograph on wove paper, 1825–1828. 13¼ x
9¾ in. Printed on stone l.c.: *From the Original Series
painted by Stuart. / for the Messrs. Doggett of Boston.;*
l.r.: *Entered according to the Act of Congress.*
American Antiquarian Society; gift of Charles Henry
Taylor.

**36   James Madison, Fourth President of the United
States.**
Crayon lithograph on wove paper, 1825–1828. 13¾ x
9¾ in. Printed on stone l.c.: *From the Original Series
painted by Stuart. / for the Messrs. Doggett of Boston.;*
l.r.: *Entered according to the Act of Congress.*
American Antiquarian Society; gift of Charles Henry
Taylor.

**37   James Monroe, Fifth President of the United
States.**
Crayon lithograph on wove paper, 1825–1828. 13½ x
9¾ in. Printed on stone l.c.: *From the Original Series
painted by Stuart / for the Messrs. Doggett of Boston;*
l.r.: *Entered according to the Act of Congress.*
Boston Athenæum.

This group of portraits of the first five American presidents, the "American Kings," was published by John
Doggett, the owner of a looking glass and carpet warehouse on Market Street in Boston, where he also sold
prints. In early 1822 Doggett exhibited Gilbert Stuart's
paintings of the five presidents and proposed to issue
prints of the paintings on a subscription basis. John
Pendleton must have offered to oversee the production of
the prints, as he went to Paris in 1825 and learned as
much as possible about lithography. He returned to
Boston, bringing with him lithographic stones bearing
the drawings of the presidents by a French lithographer,
as well as an experienced pressman and the equipment
needed to produce lithographs. The French lithographer
is referred to in the prospectus as "Monsieur Maurin, an
eminent lithographist of Paris."[45] Traditionally, it has
been assumed that "Monsieur Maurin" was Nicolas-
Eustache Maurin; however, his brother Antoine Maurin
(1793–1860), was working as a lithographer in Paris at
the same time.

The prospectus laid out a lavish plan for publication,
hoping to draw subscribers to the project.[46] However, in
spite of the prospectus' promises, the project languished,
perhaps because of a lack of subscribers or the antici-
pated cost of reproducing the portraits as folio engravings. John Pendleton's lack of experience also apparently
contributed to the project's failure. In the diary of
Jonathan Cobb, Doggett's son-in-law, Cobb complained
that John Pendleton "could not perform the workman-
ship," and "made divers frivolous excuses and delays."[47]
Some prints apparently were made during 1825–1826,
but whether these prints were produced earlier in France
is unclear. After a series of delays, a second attempt was
made, and the lithographs were finally executed and
printed sometime between 1826 and 1828. Although
"The American Kings" are among the finest examples of
early American lithography, many elements of the final,
successful production remain obscure.   G. B./C. S.

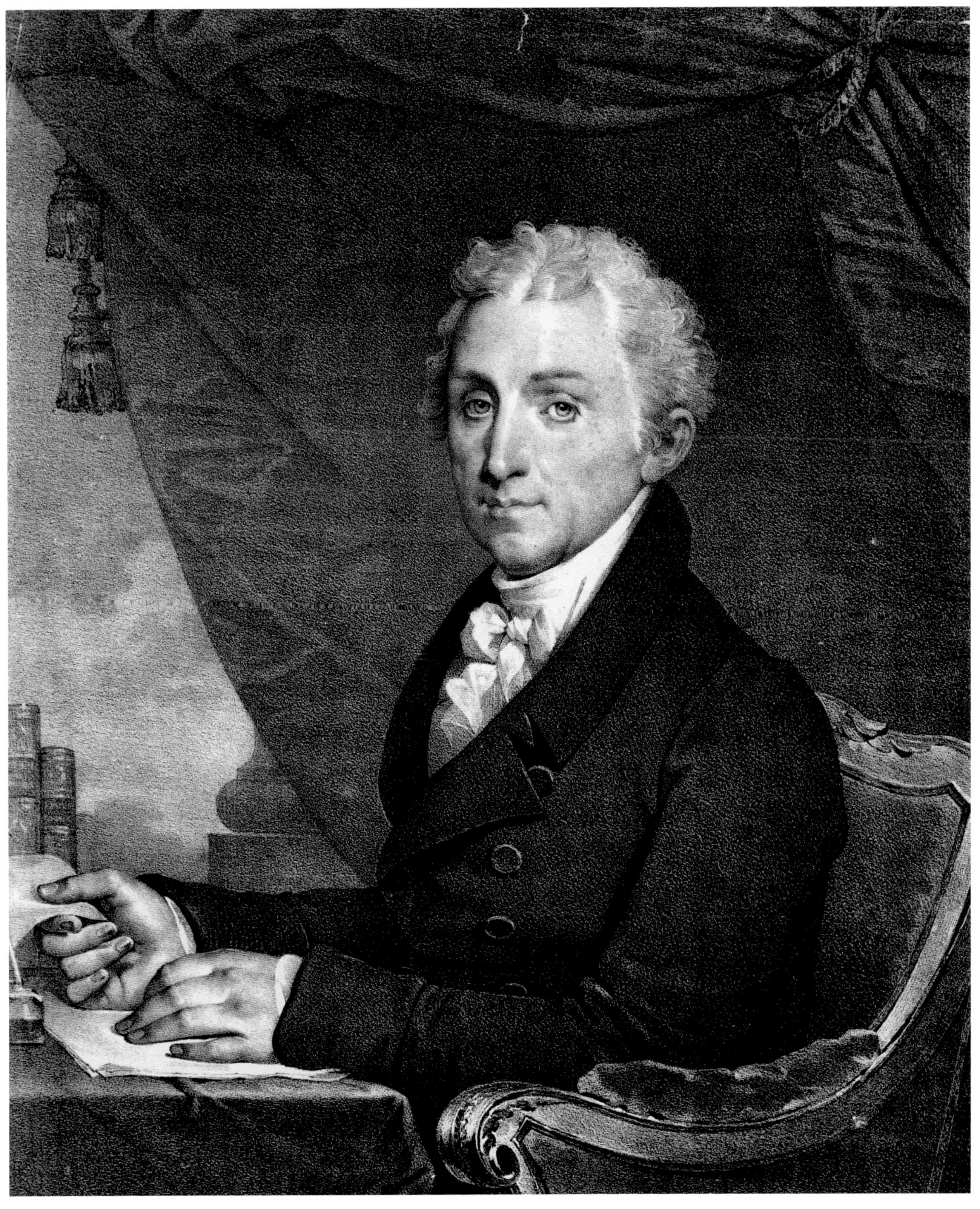

Cat. 37   Nicholas-Eustache Maurin, *James Monroe, Fifth President of the United States* (1825–1828).

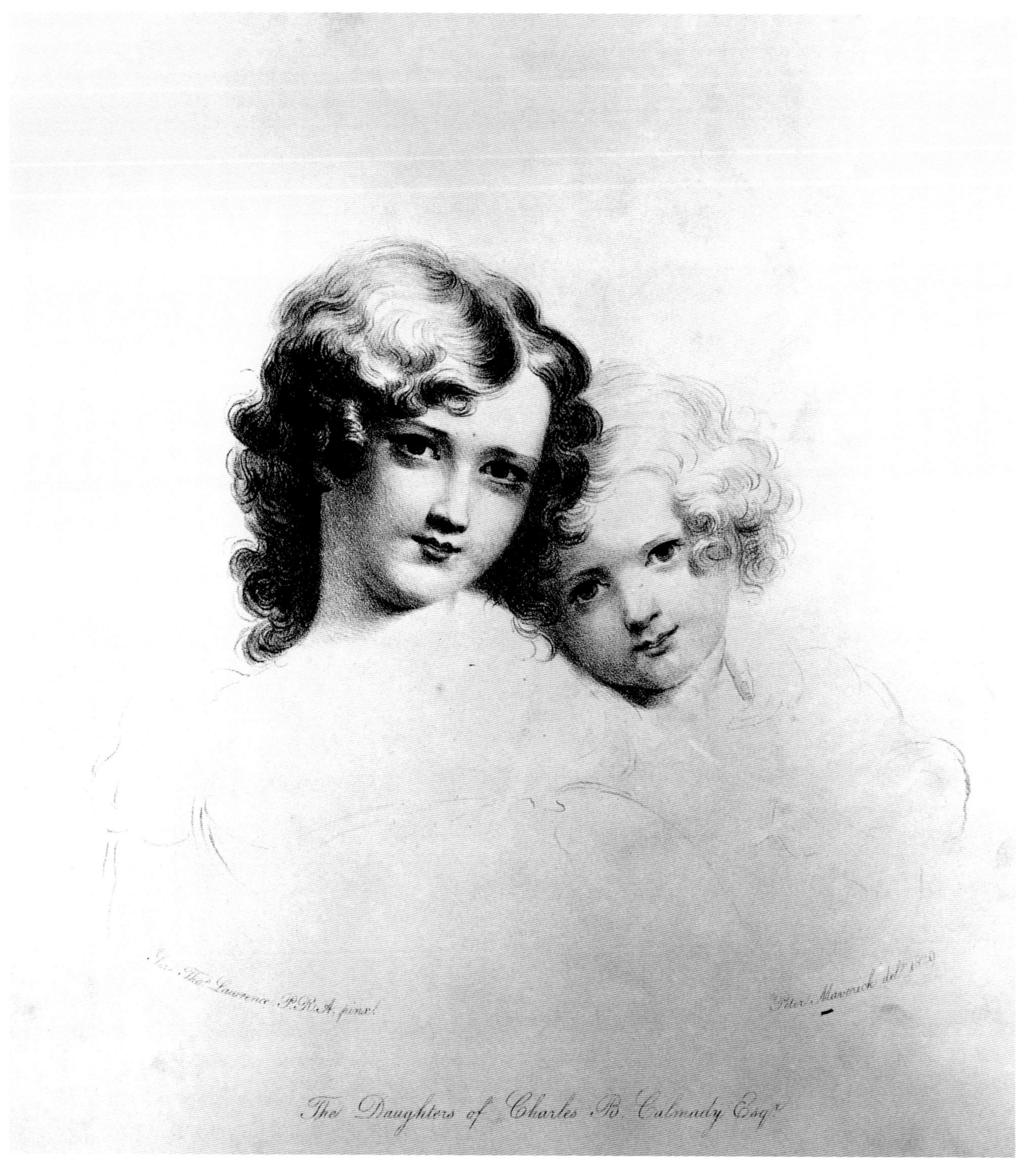

Cat. 58   Peter Maverick, *The Daughters of Charles B. Calmady* (1829).

Peter Maverick (1780–1831).

38 The Daughters of Charles B. Calmady Esqr.
Crayon lithograph on wove paper, 1829. 9 x 8 in.
Printed on stone l.l.: *Sir Thos. Lawrence. P. R. A. pinx.;*
l.r.: *Peter Maverick delt. 1829;* l.c.: *Lithy. P. Maverick
N. York.*
American Antiquarian Society.

In the summer of 1823, Sir Thomas Lawrence
(1769–1830) was commissioned to paint the young
daughters of Charles Biggs Calmady of Devonshire.
Lawrence was enchanted by the children and drew several preliminary sketches. The finished oil painting was
exhibited at the Royal Academy in 1824, and received
accolades from all quarters. English and French lithographs were quickly produced and widely circulated. The
painting had universal appeal: the King of England "was
very desirous of possessing it," and lithographic copies
were "to be found throughout the provincial towns and . . .
farmhouses" of France.[48]

Peter Maverick's lithograph, however, was based on
Lawrence's initial oil sketch for the painting. Whereas the
finished painting showed the youngest daughter in full-
length and the older child in profile, the sketch presented
just the heads of the sisters in full face. According to
Lawrence's first biographer, D. E. Williams, this preliminary sketch was vastly superior to the oil painting: "A
more free, masterly, and exquisitely beautiful sketch was
scarcely ever made... both of the faces were . . . rich and
lovely and more soft and delicate than in the finished picture."[49] The study was popularized by an 1825 engraving
by British printmaker Frederick Christian Lewis
(1779–1856).

The image struck a chord on this side of the Atlantic
as well. In addition to Maverick's lithograph, the Pendleton
firm subsequently produced its own lithographic version,
called *The Sisters.* As the more generic title implies, the
image transcended its origin as a portrait and became in the
popular imagination an idealization of childhood.   C. S.

Louisa Davis Minot (1788–1858).

39 View On the Kennebeck At Gardiner.
Crayon lithograph on wove paper, ca. 1826. 8 x 10½ in.
Printed on stone l.l.: *L. M. del.;* l.r.: *Lith. of Pendleton*
[Boston].
American Antiquarian Society.

Signed with the initials "L. M.," this print can be attributed to Louisa Davis Minot, who was well acquainted
with Mrs. Robert Hallowell Gardiner of Gardiner,
Maine. In a letter to her husband from Gardiner, dated

October 5, 1824, Louisa wrote of a "pleasant sketching
excursion."[50] On April 8, 1826, she sent Mrs. Gardiner a
lithograph, with a note reading in part, "I am desirous of
availing myself of so good an opportunity, to send you my
first attempts at Lithographic drawing. They have so little merit that I should not venture to send them to you, if
I were not aware how interested you are in the art and
how indulgent to the most imperfect efforts . . . It is very
easy to learn to draw on the stone, but it takes more time
and requires more nicety than drawing in pencil. If Emma
[apparently Mrs. Gardiner's daughter] should be inclined
to try it, there will be no difficulty in transporting the
stones from this place to Gardiner and back again to be
struck off."[51]   G. B.

Rembrandt Peale (1778–1860).

40 Lord Byron.
Crayon lithograph on wove paper, 1826. 11¾ x 9 in.
Printed on stone l.l.: *R. Peale del;* l.r.: *Litho. of
Pendleton* [Boston].
Boston Athenæum; gift of Charles E. Mason, Jr., 1977.

This is the second of two lithographic portraits of Lord
Byron created by the American artist Rembrandt Peale.
The earlier version, Peale's first attempt at lithography,
was made in New York in 1825, and seems to have served
principally as a study for this second version, which was
produced in Boston in large quantities for commercial
sale.[52] Both versions were based on the British painter
Richard Westall's (1765–1836) 1813 life portrait of the
poet (now in London's National Portrait Gallery). Shortly
after Westall's painting was completed, engraved copies
of the portrait were made by several British engravers,
including the well-known Charles Turner, which were
widely circulated and probably were the source of Peale's
acquaintance with Westall's portrait.

Peale's lithograph differs in one substantial way from
the Westall portrait. Westall painted Lord Byron with his
elbow resting on a rock; Peale has done away with the
rock and added the sheaf of manuscripts in the lower left
corner. Peale obviously felt entitled to such artistic license.
He felt strongly that printmaking was an art of equal
value to that of oil painting. He wrote, "When copies are
made by able Artists, either from their own works, or those
of others, their merit may be nearly equal, sometime
superior to the originals . . ."[53]

In Peale's lithograph, Lord Byron is portrayed as a
dashing, handsome romantic. But an American acquaintance of Byron wrote that "his face [was] not finely
shaped, being inclined to be broad and flat. In this
respect, the best prints have flattered him; or at least the

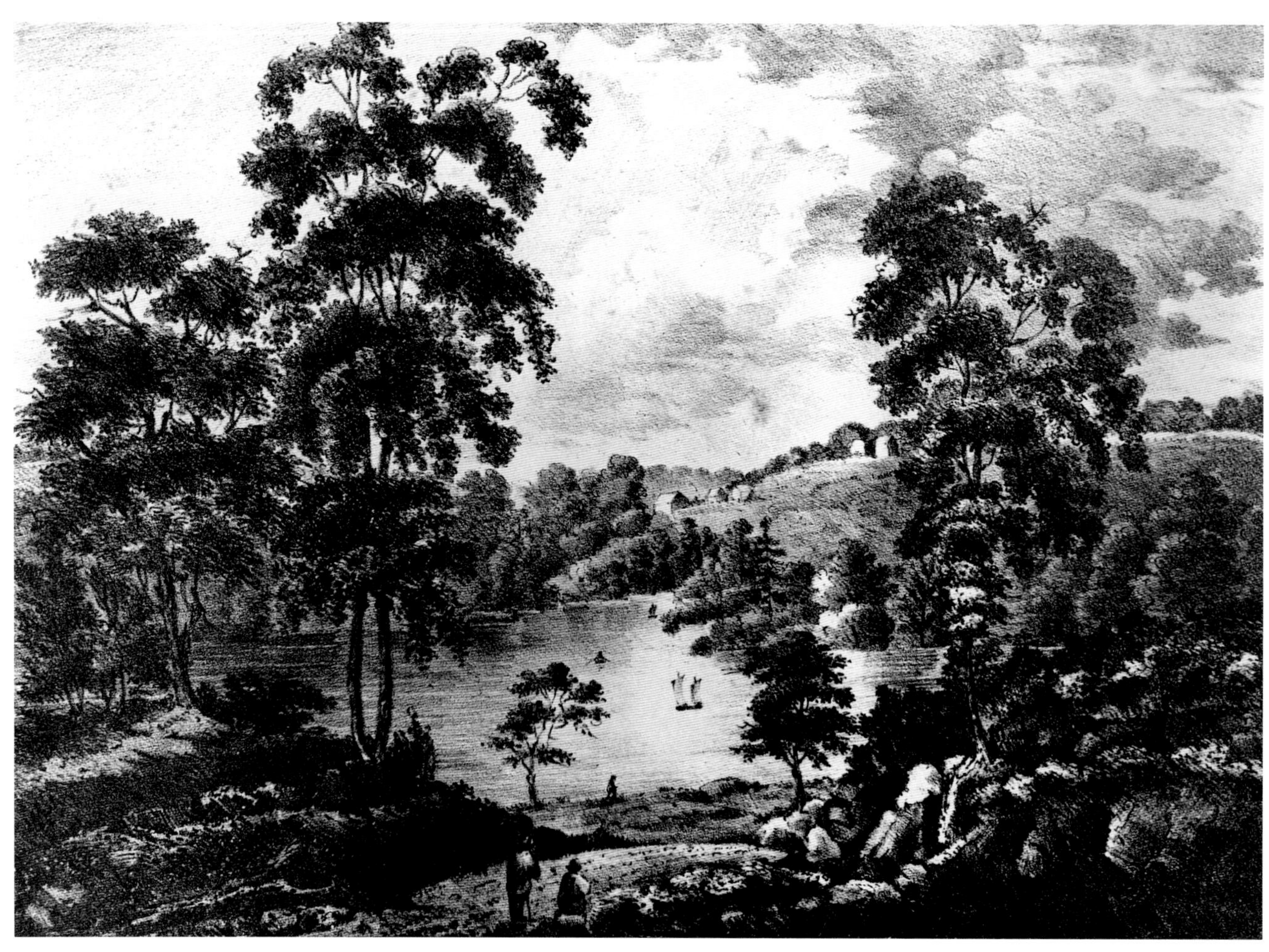

Cat. 39   Louisa Minot, *View on the Kennebeck at Gardiner* (ca. 1826).

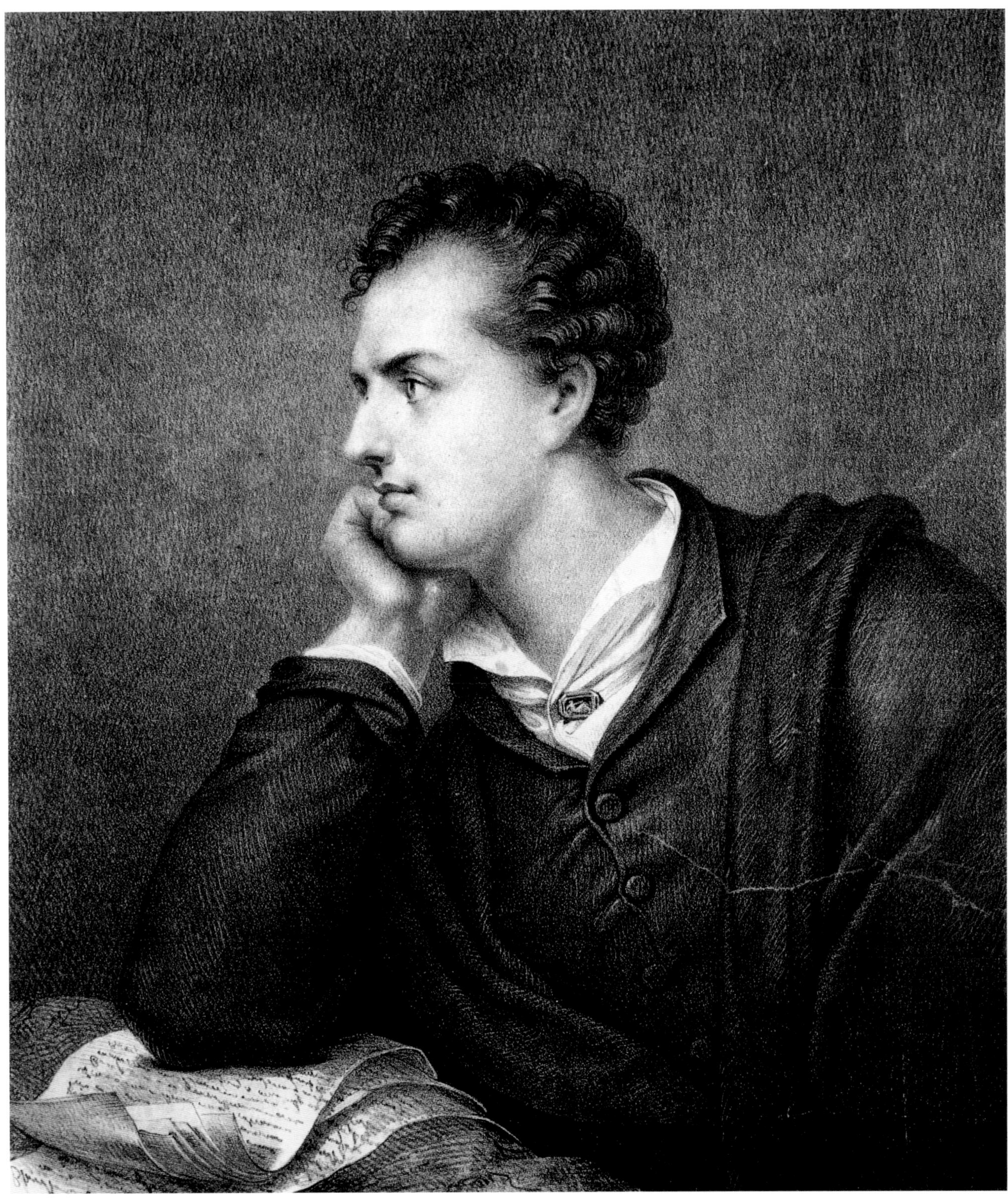

Cat. 40   Rembrandt Peale, *Lord Byron* (1826).

profile, which they exhibit, was better that the front face. His eye was a dark grey, mild and soft; his nose somewhat broad; the lips full, the upper lip considerably arched, and his smile singularly winning. The chin was marked with a dimple, but bold and finely turned. The line in his face from the chin to the ear has always been remarked as uncommonly beautiful . . . "[54]

In the January 1825 edition of Boston's erudite literary journal the *North American Review,* Lord Bryon's untimely death from malaria in 1824 was called "a public calamity" (p. 2), and "without depressing the price of stocks . . . has produced a deep and general feeling of regret throughout the country" (p. 1). In discussing Byron and his poetry, the *North American Review* evinced the same ambivalence that the poet inspired in the general public. On the one hand, "he certainly appeared to the world as one of the most favored and enviable beings in creation" (p. 7), and yet "the leaning of Lord Byron is . . . decidedly immoral" (p. 43).

Rembrandt Peale (1778–1860).

41   **Patriae Pater.**
Crayon lithograph on wove paper, 1827. 21¾ x 15½ in. Printed on stone l.l.: *Drawn on Stone by Rembrandt Pea[le]*; l.c.: *Copy-right secured. 1827.*; l.r.: *Pendleton's Lithography. Boston.*; l.c.: *Washington. / From the Original Portrait Painted by Rembrandt Peale.*
Boston Athenæum; Washington Fund purchase, 1990.

This lithograph was drawn on stone by Rembrandt Peale and is an exact replica of the *Senatorial Portrait,* his celebrated 1824 oil painting in the United States Senate Collection. This work was unique in the annals of American art in the mid-1820s. It was neither a life portrait, an imagined portrait, nor a copy of a life portrait, but rather a compilation of many life paintings and sculptures. Peale repeatedly referred to the painting as the "Standard National Likeness." As can be seen from the catalogue illustration, the portrait depicts Washington in American senatorial robes and dramatically surrounded by oval masonry. Peale's President appears as a majestic national father, a godhead who is both remote and intimate at the same time.

Peale's life-long obsession with Washington began when, as a child of eight, he assisted his father, the distinguished painter Charles Willson Peale (1741–1827), with his life portraits of Washington. Washington, a close friend of the senior Peale, sat for him at least fourteen times. The younger Peale was present at many of those sittings and developed "the greatest veneration for his character as well as his sublime aspect."[55] In September of 1795, Washington consented to sit for the eighteen-year-old

Rembrandt Peale and the result was a bust-length portrait of the President.

Over the years, Peale became dissatisfied with his initial portrait and other well known images of Washington such as Gilbert Stuart's portrait, Houdon's bust, and even his father's numerous portraits. In 1823, he stated that "the image of Washington once more rose to engross my mind."[56] He believed that if he combined all the various virtues of the best of the Washington portraits, he could create a genuine and "truthful likeness," the definitive portrait of the late President. Accordingly, he retired to his Philadelphia studio surrounded by "every Portrait, Bust, Medallion and Print of Washington that I could find — thus to excite and resuscitate my memory."[57] For three months he remained secluded in his studio: "I grew thin and pale . . . forgetful of time and everything else."[58] His wife worried about his "absorbing studies . . . and entreated that I would disturb my spirit no more with Washington, saying that she thought him my evil genius, and, with tears on her cheeks, wished that he never had been born!" Even his father pronounced his infatuation "a waste of time."[59] Yet the result of this "infatuation" and three months of seclusion was the *Senatorial Portrait,* probably the best known and most frequently reproduced of all his paintings.

Upon finishing the painting, Peale rushed off to Washington, D.C. to show it to Congress. He gathered letters of praise, "testimonials" from numerous dignitaries such as Chief Justice Marshall, who exclaimed, "It seems as if I were looking on the living man! It is more like him than any thing I have ever seen."[60] These "testimonials" and Peale's unabashed self promotion drew severe criticism from his contemporaries in the art community. Nonetheless, after exhibiting the painting in London, Rome, and Florence, the United States Government by unanimous vote purchased the painting from Peale for the unprecedented sum of two thousand dollars — an enormous sum at the time.

In 1826, Peale arrived in Boston to "devote myself for sometime to lithographic studies."[61] The lithograph of the *Senatorial Portrait* was known as *Patriae Pater,* and earned Peale the silver medal from the prestigious Franklin Institute. It was cited for being the "best specimen of American lithography ever seen by the committee on fine arts."[62] Peale later wrote that "Unfortunately, the workmen, by some neglect, destroyed this drawing on the stone when but a few impressions were taken."[63]

In the 1850s, Peale gave a series of Washington lectures in which he stated that his life goal was to "multiply the Countenance of Washington."[64] In addition to this lithograph, countless engravings were made of the portrait,

62

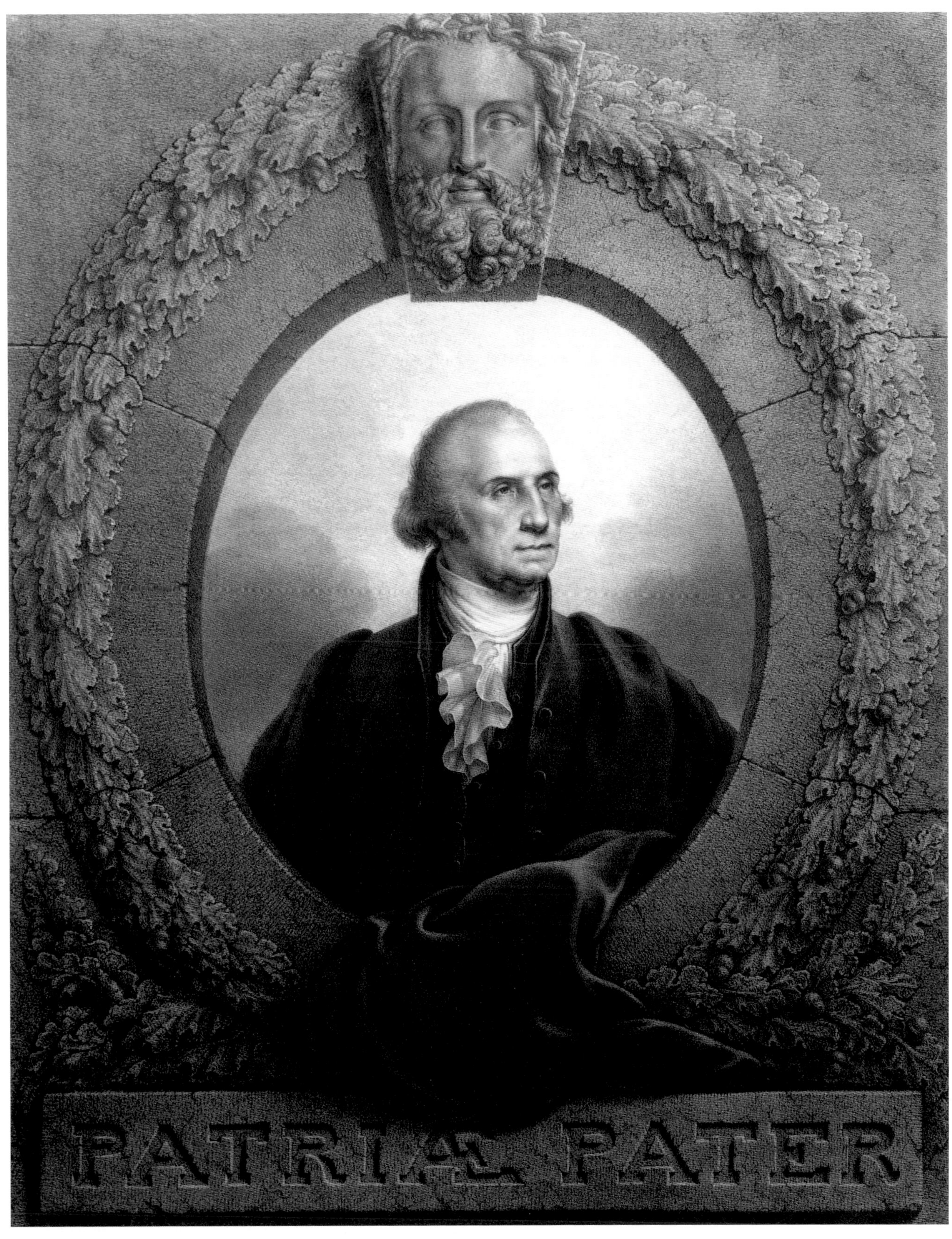

Cat. 41   Rembrandt Peale, *Patriae Pater* (1827).

some in civilian or military dress, and Peale himself copied the *Senatorial Portrait* in oil a total of seventy-nine times.   C. S.

Rembrandt Peale (1778–1860).

42   Uncut Proof Sheet For "Lithographic Sketches. Memoranda of Form & Character."
Crayon lithograph on wove paper, ca. 1828. 11¼ x 15 in. [Boston: Pendleton Lithographic Firm].
American Antiquarian Society.

Lithographic Sketches. Memoranda of Form and Character was a small pamphlet containing eight lithographs on separate pages and a letterpress caption printed beneath each image. This uncut proof for *Lithographic Sketches* is a rare survivor, with all eight images on one single sheet. On the verso is a pencil inscription that reads: "Rembrandt Peale. Printed by Pendleton. Presswork by John W. A. Scott, Stone made about 1828." One of the images, *The Soldier's Birth-Right,* is derived from a lithograph by Nicholas Toussaint Charlot (1792–1845) entitled *Y dit que vous avez une jambe de bois de naissance.*[65] Undoubtedly the other images are likewise derived from other prints.   G. B.

Catherine Scollay (1783–1863).

43   Fourth View of Trenton Falls.
Crayon lithograph on wove paper, 1826. 10¾ x 12¼ in. Printed on stone l.c.: *C. S. del. — Lithography of Pendleton* [Boston].
American Antiquarian Society.

Catherine Scollay was the daughter of William Scollay (1756–1809) of Boston, who was active as a druggist before turning to real estate. She undoubtedly learned to draw as part of her education.

Scollay drew six views of the Trenton Falls on stone in 1826. The clouds of mist above the tumbling falls in the *Fourth View of Trenton Falls* suggest the power of the water. The small figures on the left bank are dwarfed by the trees. The technical excellence of this lithograph was acknowledged by the Franklin Institute of Philadelphia, which awarded the print a Premium in its 1826 competition, citing the lithograph as "one of the best landscape paintings on stone"[66] they had ever seen. William and John Pendleton received the silver medal in that year for the excellence of their lithographs.   G. B.

John Rubens Smith (1775–1849).

44   [Mrs. J. R. Smith].
Pen lithograph on wove paper, ca. 1821–1822.
9 x 6¾ in. Printed on stone on image l.r.: *J R Smith / Lithograph;* l.l. below image: *From the Lithographic Press of Barnet & Doolittle / No. 23 Lumber Street New York.*
American Antiquarian Society.

The subject of this remarkable lithograph is quite possibly the artist's wife. Dressed in a loose-fitting, high-waisted gown and posed in a garden setting, she gazes off to the viewer's right. The freedom of the drawing suggests that the artist was drawing the portrait from life, not copying it from another work.

Smith was born in London, the son of a mezzotint engraver, and was already well established as an artist before he immigrated to the United States in 1809. He lived in Boston before moving to Brooklyn, New York, in 1814, where he established a drawing academy. He was one of the few artists to experiment with lithography in New York in 1821 and 1822, when Barnet & Doolittle were active. Indeed, Godefroy Engelmann wrote in his *Manuel du lithographe* that one reason that firm failed was the lack of artists in New York to experiment with the process.[67]   G. B.

Moses Swett (1804–1838).

45   Arcade, Providence.
Crayon lithograph with hand-coloring on wove paper, 1829. 11¼ x 14 in. Printed on stone l.l.: *M. Swett Invt. et Del.;* l.r.: *Pendletons Lithography;* l.c.: *Entered According to Act of Congress the 26th of March 1829 By W. & J. Pendleton Boston, Mass.*
Boston Athenæum.

The Arcade was built in 1828 in Providence, Rhode Island, and was a very early example of what is now called a shopping mall. At one time, this three-story granite building had twenty-six retail shops on each floor. Clothing stores were particularly popular.

The Arcade was a large transept-shaped building: half of it fronted on Westminster Street and was owned by Cyrus Butler; the other half faced Weybosset Street and belonged to the Arcade Realty Company. To design the two entrances, the owners hired the architectural firm of Warren and Bucklin. Russell Warren, an early advocate of the Greek Revival style, worked for the Arcade corporation and designed the Weybosset Street entrance shown here with its six Ionic columns and a parapet. Bucklin created a slightly different facade for the Westminster

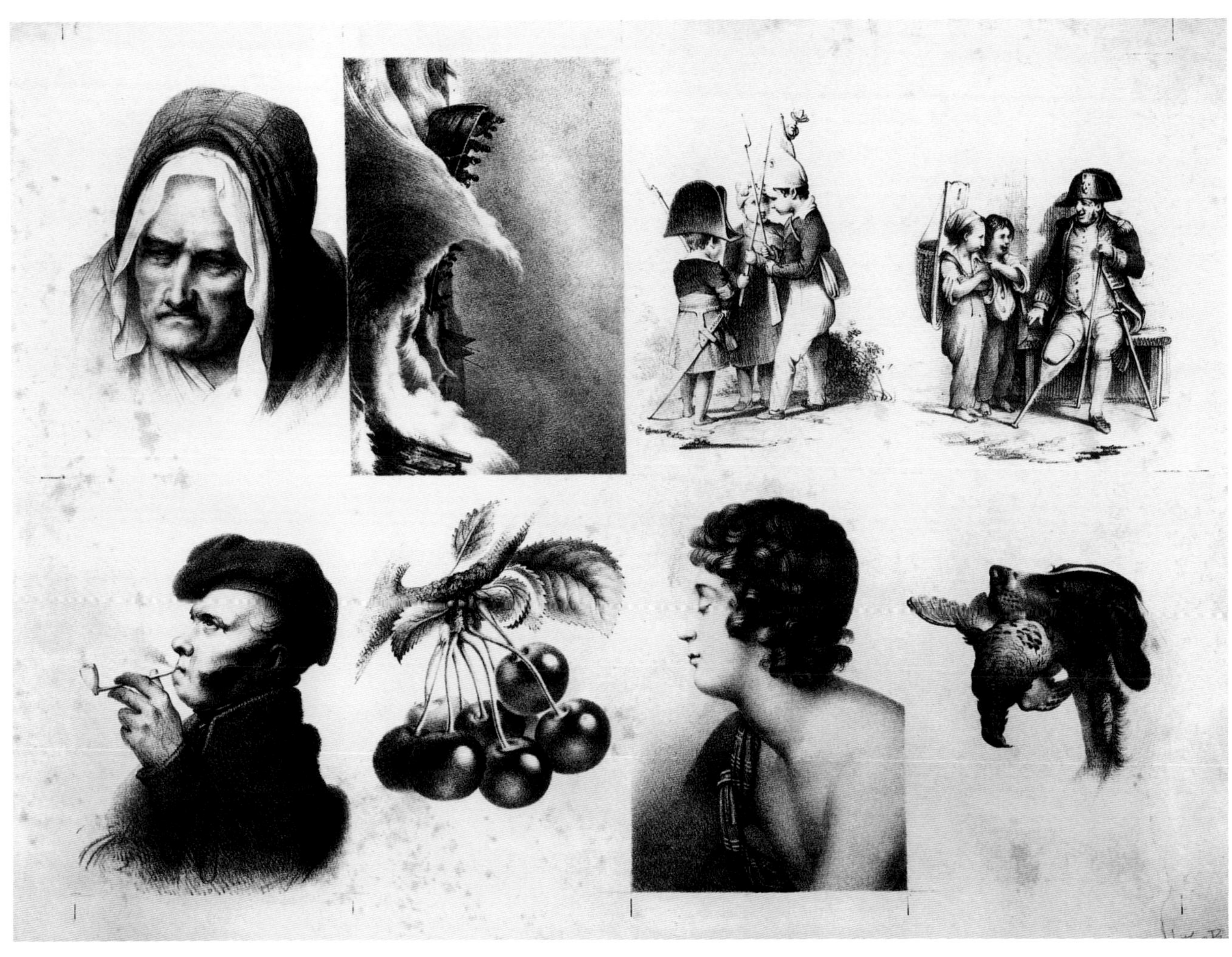

Cat. 42   Rembrandt Peale, Uncut Proof Sheet for *"Lithographic Sketches. Memoranda of Form & Character"* (ca. 1828).

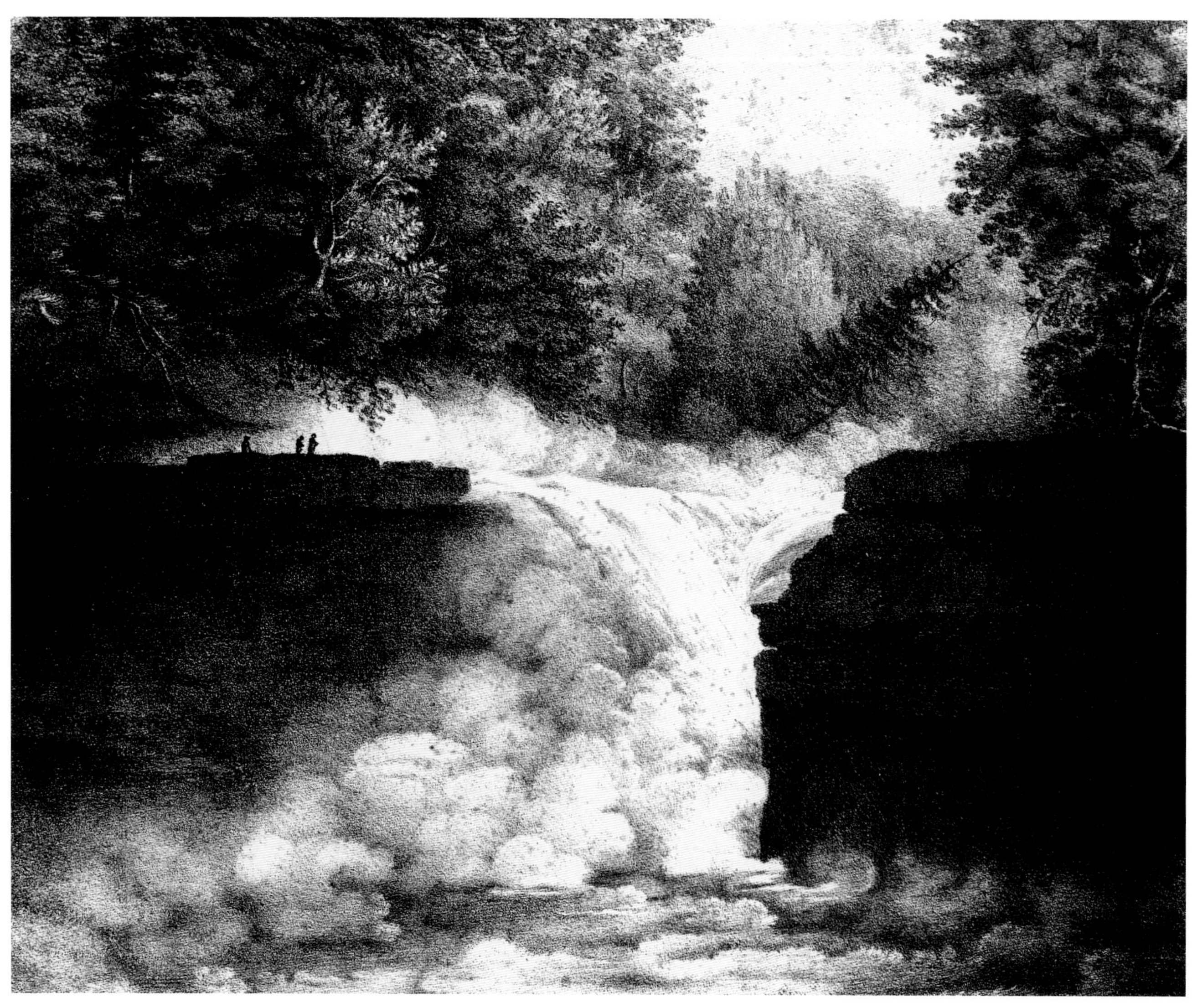

Cat. 43   Catherine Scollay, *Fourth View of Trenton Falls* (1826).

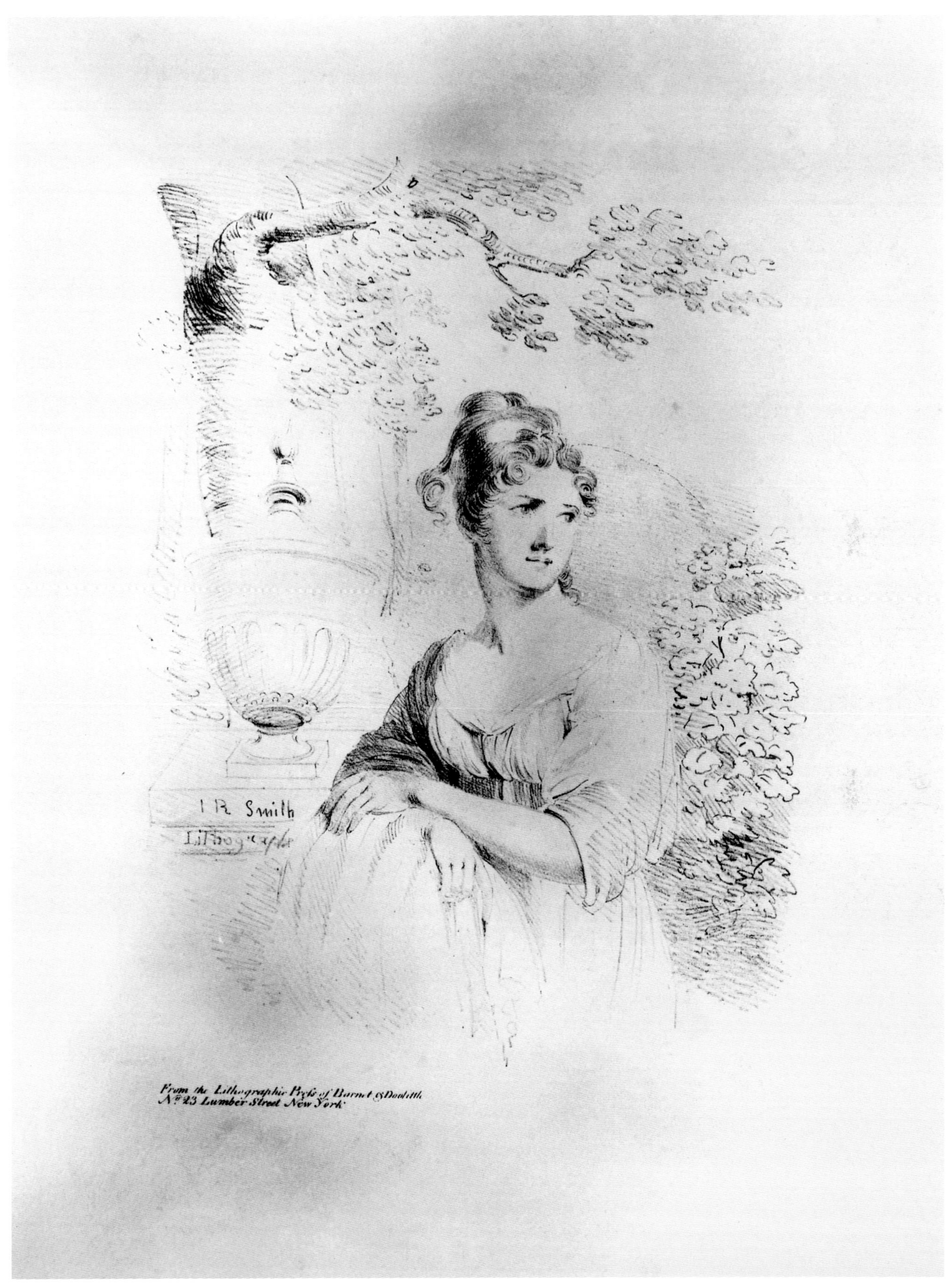

Cat. 44 John Rubens Smith, [*Mrs. J. R. Smith*] (ca. 1821–1822).

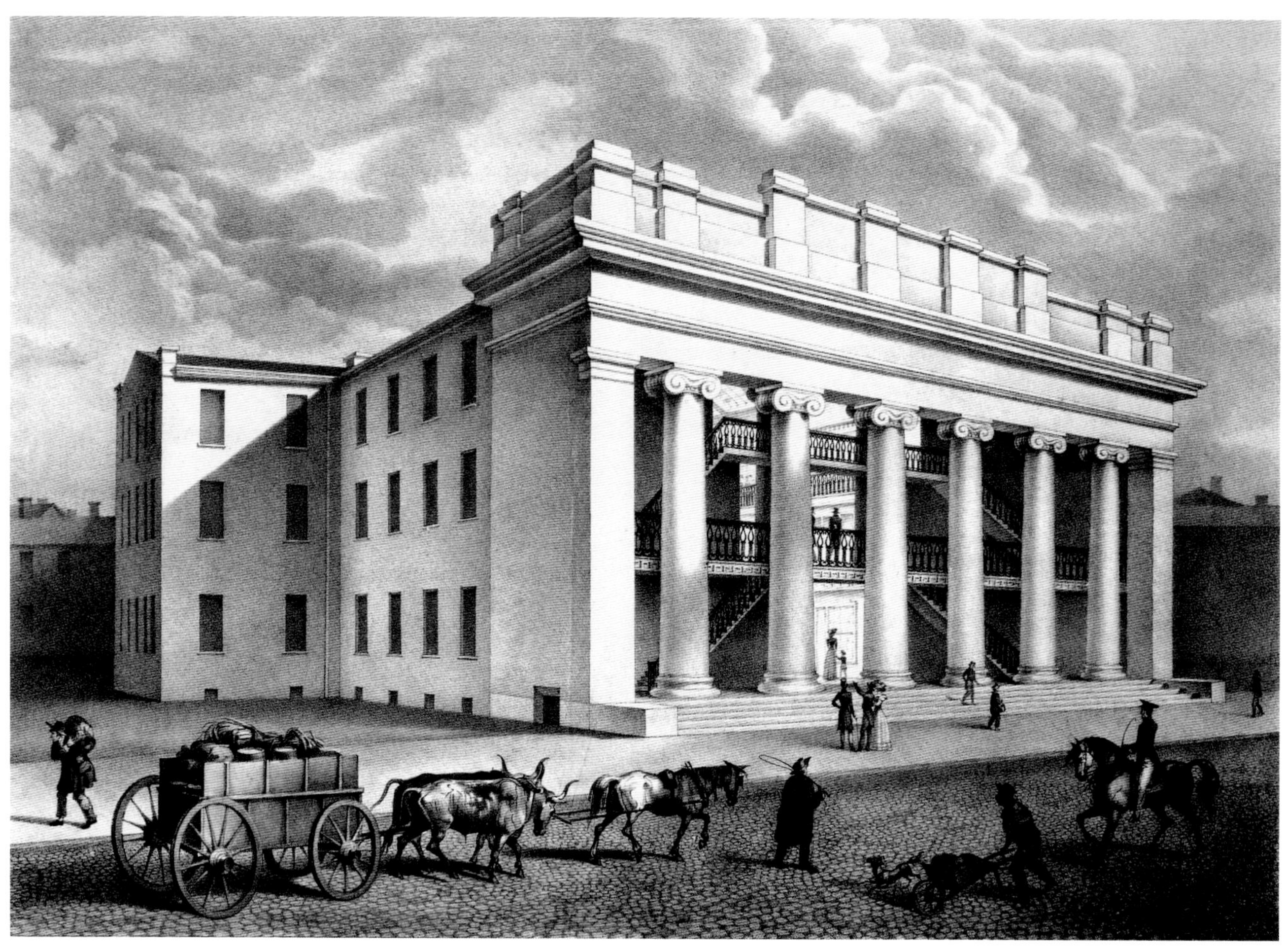

Cat. 45   Moses Swett, *Arcade, Providence* (1829).

street entrance. Stone staircases were at either end of the buildings, and each floor had corridors connecting the two halves. The central court was covered with a glass roof. The Arcade was not as profitable as the owners desired, but it was considered "the most beautiful building in Providence and one that exceeds all others in the United States devoted to the same objects."[68]   C. S.

Moses Swett (1804–1838).

46 The Battle of Lexington.
Crayon and pen lithograph on white wove paper, ca. 1828. 13 x 15½ in. Printed on stone l.l.: *M Swett Invt & del.;* l.r.: *Pendletons Lithography Boston.*
Boston Athenæum; gift of Charles E. Mason, Jr., 1984.

Moses Swett carefully noted that he was the "inventor" of this image — *"M Swett Invt & del."* Yet the lithograph is clearly based on Amos Doolittle's (1754–1832) popular 1775 engraving of the Battle of Lexington. Like Doolittle's engraving, Swett's lithograph depicts Lexington Common with Buckman's Tavern on the left, the central Meeting House, and the belfry on the right. The viewpoint is also identical: the minutemen are shown in the right foreground and the British infantry, led by Major John Pitcairn, are positioned directly in the center of the print.

Yet for all their similarities, there are some crucial differences between Swett's 1828 lithograph and Doolittle's 1775 engraving. Doolittle and the painter Ralph Earl (1785–1801) visited Lexington a month after the battle in order to prepare a visual documentation of the event based on eyewitness testimony. The final engraving was made in a country torn by violence and revolutionary fervor, and Doolittle's primary motive was to provide his fellow countrymen with timely information about the carnage in Lexington. Consequently, his engraving shows the minutemen in considerable disarray: several men lie dead or wounded and the rest are fleeing the gunfire of the British. The Lexington farmers are clearly victims of a large and ruthless British army.

Swett created his lithographic version over fifty years later. By 1828 the Battle of Lexington had become a legendary historical event and he could afford to take a more dispassionate approach. His lithograph presents the minutemen as valiant and courageous, their dress more elegant and their general state of composure striking in contrast to Doolittle's bewildered yeomen. They are no longer merely victims, but heroes actively engaged in the battle. Skirting the issue of historical accuracy, Swett has depicted several farmers firing their rifles into the advancing British army.

Swett's composition, with its carefully rendered figures and its attention to spatial distances, is the more polished and artistically accomplished of the two images. The differences between the two prints arise from the fact that Doolittle's engraving was created to convey information to a besieged populace, while Swett's lithograph celebrated a past national event and was intended to hang in the homes of prosperous and genteel Americans.   C. S.

Moses Swett (1804–1838).

47 [Massachusetts Humane Society Certificate].
Crayon lithograph on white wove paper, ca. 1827–1828. 10 x 8¾ in. Printed on stone beneath image l.l.: *M. Swett, invt. et Del.;* l.r.: *Lith. of Pendleton* [Boston].
Boston Athenæum purchase, 1992.

The Humane Society of the Commonwealth of Massachusetts petitioned the state for incorporation in 1791, stating that "it is the duty of government at all times, to countenance and support its citizens, in their exertions for alleviating the distresses of their fellow-men." The petition clearly articulated the Society's mission: "the recovery of persons who meet with such accidents as produce in them the appearance of death, and . . . pursuing such means . . . as shall have for their object, the preservation of human life, and the alleviation of its miseries."[69]

From its conception, the Society devoted much of its energy to educating the public about "the method of treatment to be used with persons apparently dead from drowning."[70] In this lithograph, one of the rescuers holds a bottle in his hand as he rushes towards the victim, demonstrating the Society's injunction that "the body is to be . . . sprinkled with spirits, and fomentations of hot rum are to be applied to the breast . . . and often renewed."[71]

One of the functions of the Society was to reward people who saved, or attempted to save, "the life of a citizen of this commonwealth,"[72] and medals, certificates and occasionally pecuniary rewards were presented at the Society's meetings. This particular certificate was awarded with a silver medal on the fourth of December, 1829, to Captain Benjamin Oliver, who, with two other men, attended the scene of a shipwreck.[73] The incident was described in the September 26, 1829, edition of the *Columbian Centinel:* "It being apparent that the wreck must soon sink with the men, and there being no other way to preserve their lives but by the risk of life, Capt. Benj. Oliver, Elisha B. Wesherell and Elisha H. Baker, all of Wellfleet, volunteered to go in the boat and succeeded in saving the whole four from a watery grave . . ."   C. S.

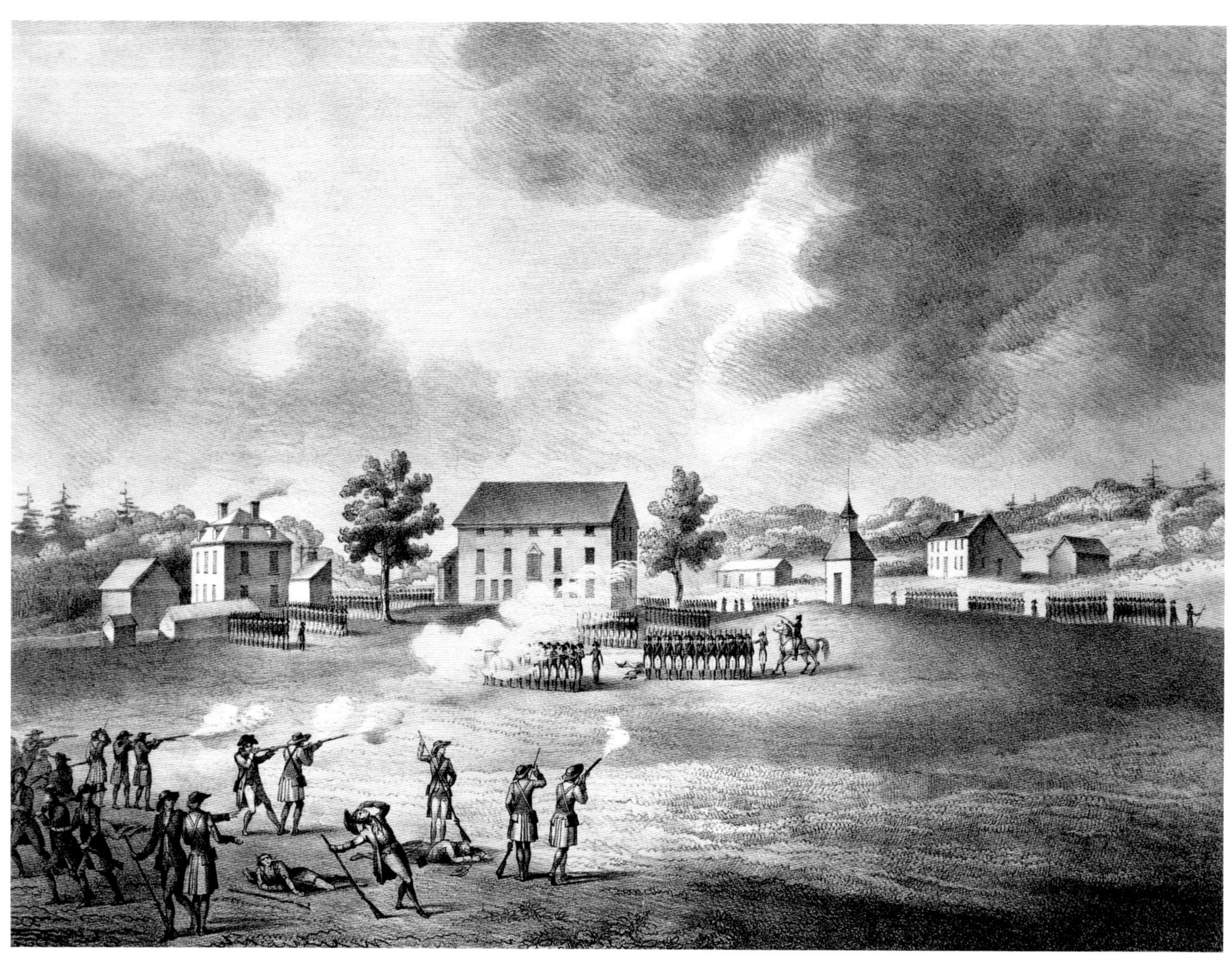

Cat. 46   Moses Swett, *Battle of Lexington, 1775* (ca. 1828).

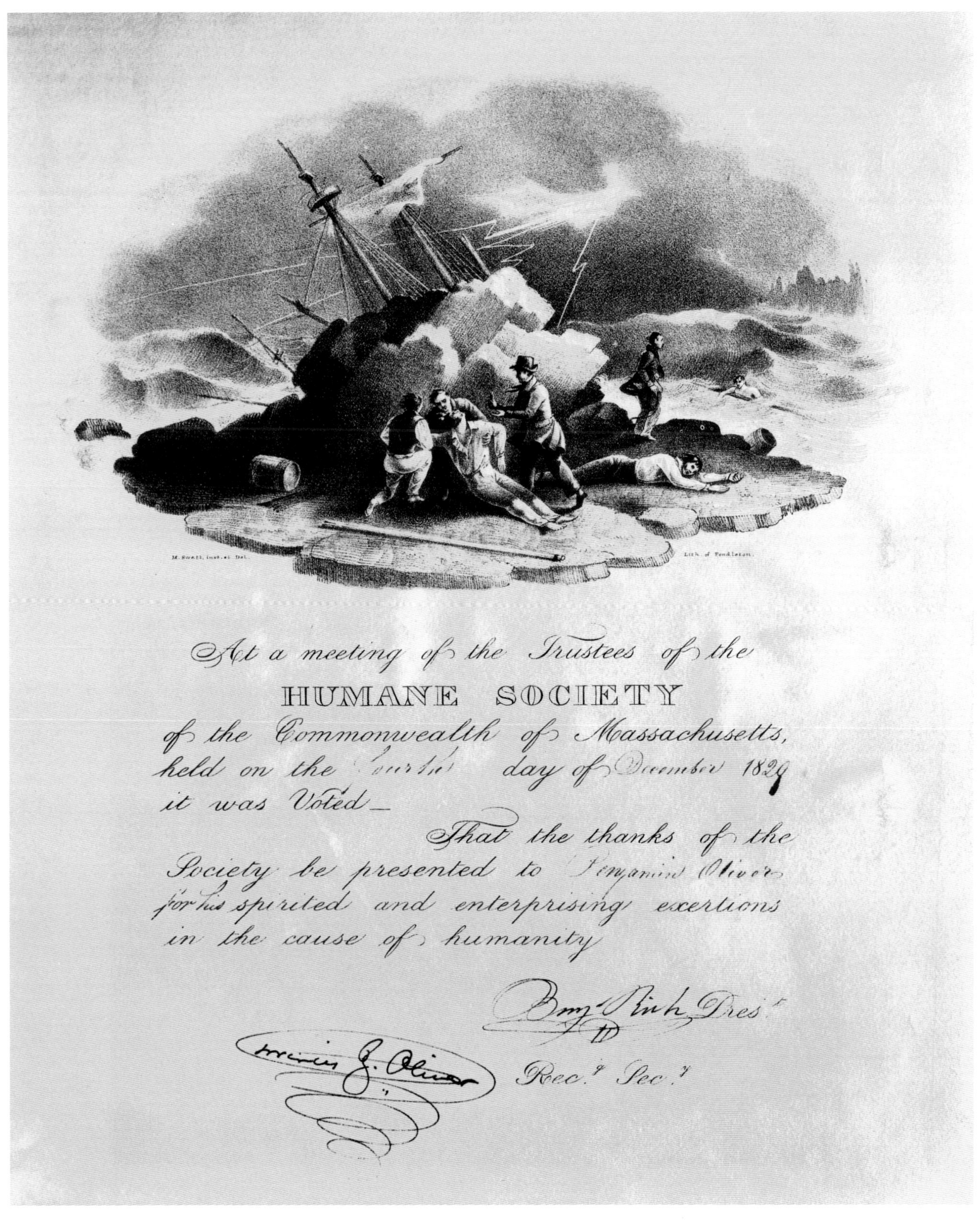

Cat. 47   Moses Swett, *Massachusetts Humane Society Certificate* (ca. 1827–1828).

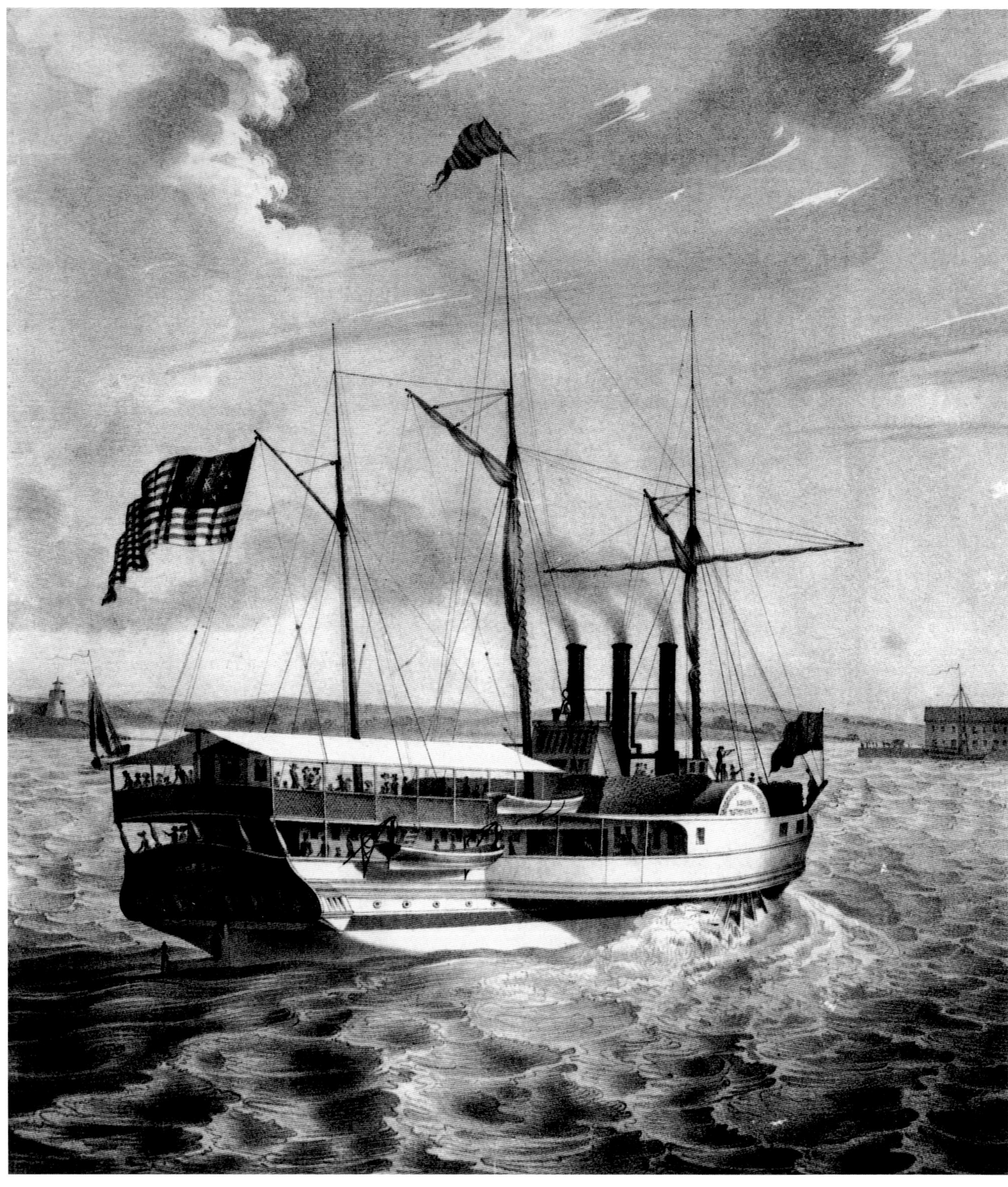

Cat. 48 Moses Swett, *Steam Packet "Chancellor Livingston"* (ca. 1828).

72

Moses Swett (1804–1838).

48 Steam Packet Chancellor Livingston (Entering the Harbour of Newport).
Crayon lithograph on wove paper, ca. 1828.
14½ x 11¼ in. Printed on stone l.l.: *M. Swett, Invt. et Del.*; l.r.: *Pendleton's Lithog.ʸ Boston.*
Boston Athenæum purchase, 1982.

The *Chancellor Livingston* was the last and biggest steamboat to be designed by Robert Fulton before his death. He named the boat in honor of his partner and financial backer, the diplomat and statesman Robert R. Livingston. The steamboat was built in 1816 by America's premier naval architect, Henry Eckford, and at the time of her launching she was the largest steamboat in the world, weighing nearly 500 tons and costing approximately $120,000. The North River Steamboat Company owned the *Chancellor Livingston* from 1816 to 1827; she was the most popular boat on the Hudson River, making the trip from New York to Albany an average of 170 times a year.

In 1828, the *Chancellor Livingston* was purchased by Cornelius Vanderbilt and completely refurbished. New and stronger engines were installed, along with three smoke pipes and an upper deck cabin with a protective awning. She was the first steamboat to provide three separate decks for passengers. Under Vanderbilt's ownership the boat was transferred to the Providence to New York run.

As the caption under this prints reads, the *Chancellor Livingston* could seat up to 200 passengers and offered "superior accommodations for Ladies." The fare was six dollars, and meals were available for an additional fee. In 1830, dinner was advertised for "50¢; Breakfast and Tea 38¢."[74] The *Chancellor Livingston* had a reputation for serving excellent brandy, whisky, and red wine, but after an accident occurred in 1831, Vanderbilt banned the serving of hard liquor during meals.

In 1833, the *Chancellor Livingston* was sold to the Boston & Portland Line, and this once elegant and fashionable steamboat was gradually superseded by newer and more powerful ships.   C. S.

Moses Swett (1804–1838).

49 [Trade Card For the Senefelder Press].
Crayon lithograph on wove paper, ca. 1828.
18 x 15½ in. Printed on stone in cartouche at right: *Designed and Executed in Litho. by M. Swett.*
American Antiquarian Society.

This ornamental advertisement for the Senefelder Press in Boston features a portrait of Alois Senefelder (1771–

1834), the inventor of the lithographic process. Moses Swett probably designed the trade card in 1828 when he became the superintendent of the Annin and Smith-Senefelder Lithographic Company. He had previously worked for the Pendleton firm, where he learned to draw on stone, and later became a partner in lithographic firms in Baltimore and New York. Swett was one of the most experienced and capable draftsmen of his era in Boston, as evidenced by the Cupids and landscapes on the Senefelder card, which are particularly well drawn and integrated into the elaborate rococo cartouche frame.   G. B.

J. Webb (fl. 1823–1829).

50 [Cattle].
Crayon lithograph on wove paper, 1829. 3½ x 4¾ in.
Inscribed above in manuscript: *First impression, and probably / would have been well printed / after 4 or 5 had been struck off / had not the stone been injured / by accident.* Inscribed below in manuscript: *J. Webb del. / No. 8 / February 1829 / Dixon printer Salem.*
American Antiquarian Society; gift of Charles Henry Taylor.

51 [A Mill].
Crayon lithograph on wove paper, 1828. 3 x 4¾ in.
Printed on stone l.l.: *J. Webb. del.*; on image l.c.: *No. 1.*; l.r.: *Dixon Lith.* Inscribed below in manuscript: *No. 4 / Dixon Printer / Salem / Decemr. 1828.*
American Antiquarian Society; gift of Charles Henry Taylor.

J. Webb has proven to be an elusive figure, although he is said to have been drawing portraits for the Boston engraving firm of Annin and Smith about 1823. He produced

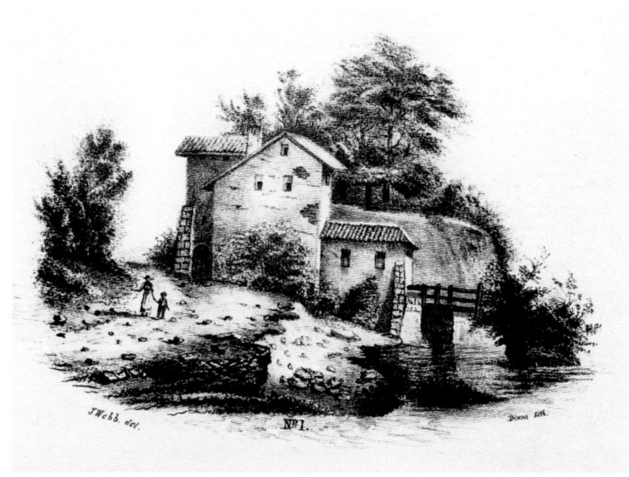

Cat. 51 J. Webb, [*A Mill*] (1828).

only eight known lithographs in 1828 and 1829, which were printed in Salem, Massachusetts, by Joseph Dixon (1799–1869), an inventor and occasional printer, and in Boston by the Senefelder Press and by the Pendleton firm. Although one of his lithographs was issued as the frontispiece to *Annot and Her Pupil,* a children's book published by Whipple & Lawrence in 1829, the others were probably printed for his private purposes as experiments. The image of the mill is derived from Plate XV in Charles Hullmandel's *The Art of Drawing on Stone* (London, 1824). The horned cattle are probably copied from some other drawing book illustration.   G. B.

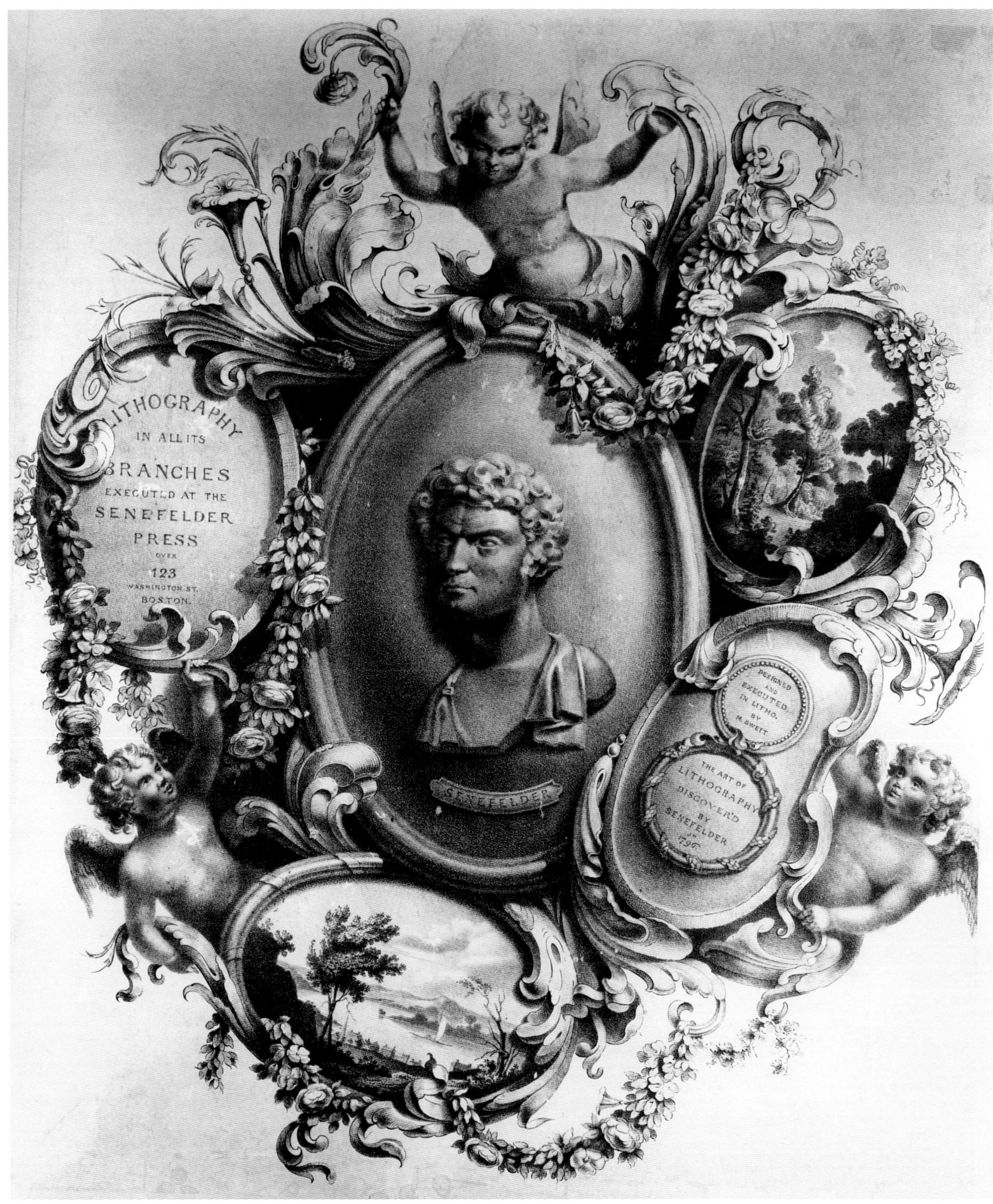

Cat. 49 Moses Swett, *Trade card for the Senefelder Press* (ca. 1828).

MUSIC

Dimensions are for image and printed text, and are rounded to the quarter inch; height precedes width.

Anonymous.

52 ***The Chaplet. A Waltz by Flora.* Philadelphia, Published by R. H. Hobson; Washington, D.C., Published by Pishey Thompson, ca. 1850.**
Pen and crayon lithograph, hand colored, on wove paper. 10 x 6½ in. Printed on stone l.c.: *Kennedy & Lucas' Lithography, No. 90 South 3rd St., Philada.*
American Antiquarian Society.

In this image a flowering espalier, its branches trained along the musical bars, rises from an ornate urn. The blossoms serve as notes and, as the text tells us, "the Bees denote Sharps." R. H. Hobson, the publisher, had a shop at 147 Chestnut Street in Philadelphia.   S. P.

Anonymous.

53 ***Frontispiece.* New York, Published by E. Riley, ca. 1824.**
Crayon and pen lithograph on white wove paper. 12¼ x 7½ in. Printed on stone l.c.: *Chanou & Desobry Lithy. 56 Exche. Place N. Y.*
American Antiquarian Society.

Intended as a frontispiece for bound volumes of sheet music, this lithograph depicts a fashionably dressed young lady who gazes directly at the viewer while playing the piano. The style of the chair and piano is French Empire.   S. P.

Anonymous.

54 ***The Mellow Horn. A very popular song composed and sung with rapturous applause, by Mr. Jones.* Boston, Published by C. Bradlee, ca. 1830.**
Crayon and pen lithograph on wove paper. 9¾ x 7¼ in. Printed on stone, l.c.: *Pendleton's Lithogy. Boston.*
Boston Athenæum; gift of Charles E. Mason, Jr., 1973.

The bold graphic quality of this cover design is unusual for its period. Within the circle of a French horn, mounted riders and hounds pursue a deer. The rising sun illuminates their chase.

John Jones (1796–1861), "a vocalist lately from London," performed "The Mellow Horn" at the Tremont Theatre, Boston, on March 26, 1830, at a benefit for himself.[75] A week later he performed it again at a benefit for Mr. Peile, a German musician.[76] This sheet music for "The Mellow Horn" is dedicated to John H. Eastburn (1805–1873), the printer for the city of Boston.   S. P.

George Loring Brown (1814–1889).

55 ***The Swiss Hunters Welcome Home. Arranged by L. Devereaux.* Boston, Published by James L. Hewitt & Co., 1829.**
Crayon and pen lithograph on wove paper. 9½ x 8½ in. Signed on stone l.l.: *G. L. B. 1829.* Printed on stone l.r.: *Senefelder Lith. Co.* [Boston].
Boston Athenæum; gift of David Tatham, 1992.

This cover, drawn by Brown when he was only fifteen years old, presents a picturesque evocation of Switzerland. A successful chamois hunter is shown returning to his wife and child and their happy home in the valley. Towering mountains, a babbling brook, and evergreen trees complete the scene.   S. P.

David Claypoole Johnston (1798–1865).

56 ***The Log House. A Song presented to the Western Minstrel by John Mills Brown.* [n.p.] 1826.**
Crayon and pen lithograph on wove paper. 11 x 8½ in. Printed on stone l.l.: *D. C. Johnston del.;* l.c.: *Copyright secured;* l.r.: *Lith. of Pendleton* [Boston].
Boston Athenæum purchase, 1982.

It is fitting that the first lithographically illustrated sheet music title page published in the United States covered a composition by Antony Philip Heinrich (1781–1861), many of whose works were inspired by American scenery or historical events. Heinrich was born in Bohemia and emigrated to the United States in 1805. In 1818, after spending some time in Philadelphia and Baltimore, he went to Bardstown, Kentucky, to seek musical inspiration in a sylvan setting. This retreat resulted in a collection of compositions entitled *The Dawning of Music in Kentucky, or, The Pleasures of Harmony in the Solitudes of Nature.* These creations were followed by many others, including the *Sylviad or Minstrelsy of Nature* of which *The Log House* formed a part. Johnston's elaborate full page cover illustration shows the composer seated outside his log cabin, trying a tune on the fiddle.   S. P.

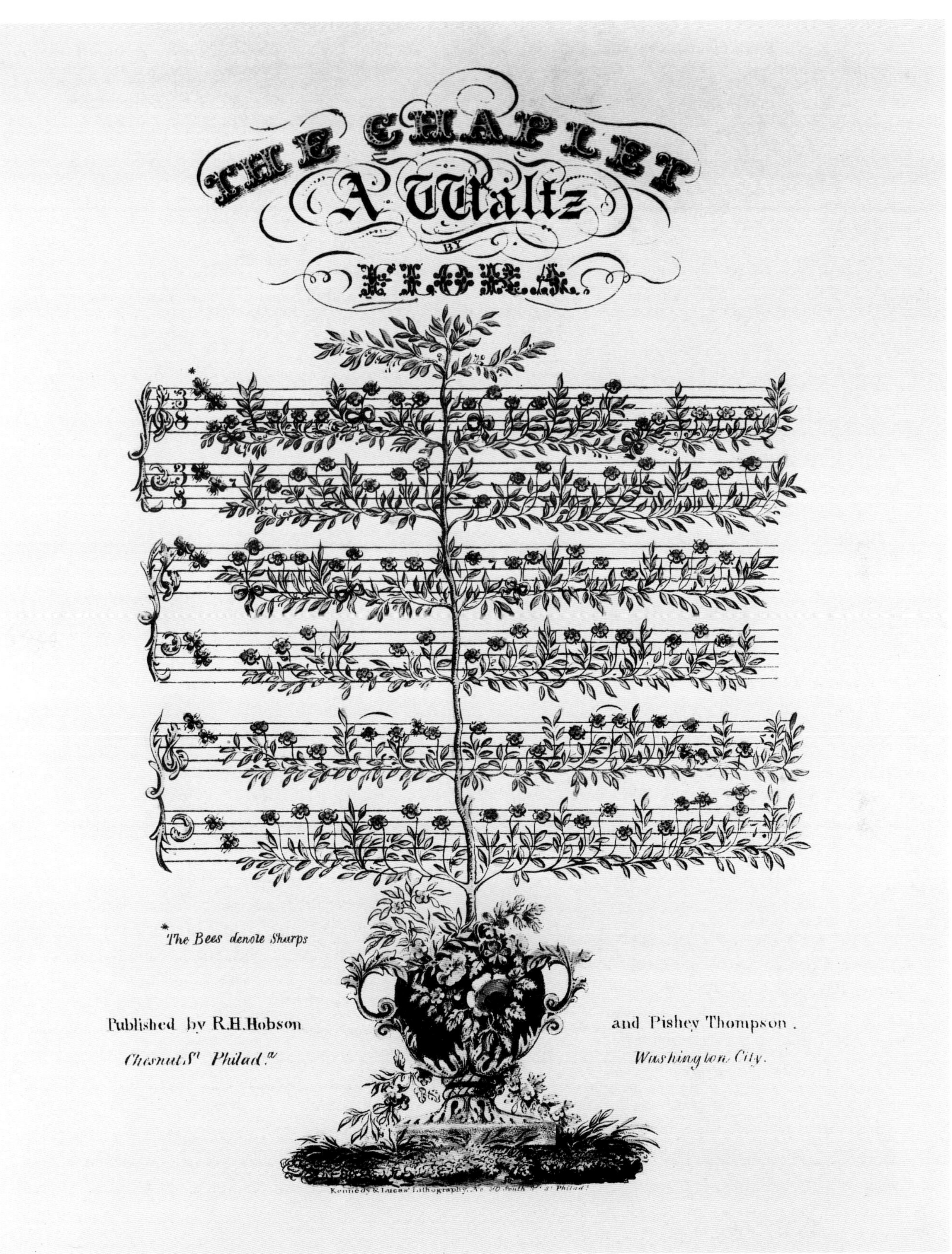

Cat. 52 Anonymous, *The Chaplet* (ca. 1830).

Stephen Henry Gimber (ca. 1806–1862).

57 *Isle of Beauty Fare Thee Well! Written by Thomas H. Bayly, Esq. The symphonies and accompaniments by T. A. Rawlings.* **New York, Published by Bourne, ca. 1829.**
Crayon and pen lithograph on yellow wove paper.
11 x 9 in. Printed on stone l.l.: *Gimber del.;* l.r.: *Lith. of Pendleton* [New York].
Boston Athenæum; gift of David Tatham, 1992.

In spirit, though not in conception or execution, Gimber's creation harks back to Watteau's *L'embarquement pour Cythère* (1717).   s. p.

Frederick Grain (fl. 1829–1857).

58 *Henry Who Adores Thee. The poetry by B. Gaites, Esqr. The music composed by T. L. Robbens.* **New York, Published by Bourne, ca. 1829.**
Crayon and pen lithograph on tan wove paper.
10¾ x 7¼ in. Printed on stone l.l.: *F. Grain del.;* l.r.: *Pendleton's Lith.* [New York].
Boston Athenæum; gift of David Tatham, 1992.

A courtship scene set in a terraced garden illustrates this love song. The English influence is evident.   s. p.

Charles Toppan (1796–1874).

59 *Rose of Love. Composed and sung by Mr. Horn, New York.* **New York, Published by A. Imbert, ca. 1828.**
Crayon and pen lithograph on wove paper.
10½ x 4¼ in. Printed on stone l.l.: *Drawn by Chas. Toppan;* l.r.: *Lithography of Imbert* [New York].
American Antiquarian Society.

Fancy female heads were frequently employed to ornament sheet music covers. This beauty is crowned with roses, and another blossom is at her waist.   s. p.

BOOKS, PERIODICALS, AND PAMPHLETS

Works are listed in chronological order by date of publication.

60 *The Analectic Magazine,* vol. 14, July 1819. **Philadelphia, Published for the Proprietor, 1819.** Boston Athenæum.

Generally considered the first lithograph published in the United States, this untitled view of a building and trees at waterside was drawn by Bass Otis (1784–1861) and is signed "Bass Otis Lithographic." Otis's technique resembles etching and aquatint, processes that he was more familiar with than the crayon manner of drawing on stone. The illustration accompanies an article on lithography detailing the pioneering experiments of Otis and others and giving instructions for various techniques of drawing and printing lithographs.

Mill scenes were popular subjects for American artists, perhaps because of the appealing combination of landscape, water, and buildings. Unfortunately, the magazine text does not reveal whether this print was drawn from nature, or derived from another source, possibly a drawing manual or a European print.   G. B.

61 *The Children's Friend,* no. 3. **New York, William B. Gilley, 1821.** American Antiquarian Society; gift of Stephen Salisbury, 1897.

Both the text and hand-colored illustrations for this charming children's book were produced lithographically. The illustrations have been attributed to Arthur J. Stansbury (1781–c. 1845), and the printing to Barnet & Doolittle, the first commercial lithographic firm in the United States. *The Children's Friend* predates Clement Moore's "A Visit from St. Nicholas" by a year. Since the two poems share common elements, such as reindeer pulling Santa Claus's sleigh and the gifts presented to the children, it seems probable that Clement Moore knew this publication.[77]   G. B.

62 *The American Journal of Science,* vol. 4, no. 2. **New Haven, Printed by S. Converse, 1822.** American Antiquarian Society.

The drawing of rock strata and fossils at the *Coal Mine of Treuil* by Jacques Gerard Milbert (1766–1840) is one of six lithographs printed by the New York firm of Barnet & Doolittle for inclusion in this volume. It accompanies an article on vegetable fossils by Alexandre Brongniart (1770–1847) first published in the *Annales des mines* for 1821 and translated by Isaac Doolittle, a partner in the lithographic firm. Elsewhere, in the *American Journal of Science,* editor Benjamin Silliman commented that the "great recommendation of lithography is the comparative cheapness and dispatch, with which designs are executed by it." He further notes that the process is "equal, if not superior, to copper plate" for the production of landscapes and natural history subjects and "for portraits it is exceedingly handsome."   G. B.

63 *Journal of the Academy of Natural Sciences of Philadelphia,* vol. 2, part 2. **Philadelphia, Printed for the Society by J. Harding, 1822.** Boston Athenæum; Bowditch Fund purchase, 1871.

This volume of the *Journal* contains two lithographs of fish, drawn on stone by Charles Alexandre Lesueur (1778–1846) and printed at the press of Barnet & Doolittle in New York. The plate of *Cichla aenea* accompanies a paper entitled "Descriptions of the Five New Species of the Genus *Cichla* of Cuvier" read by Lesueur on June 11, 1822. A drawing of *Sc. oscula* accompanies the paper "Description of Three New Species of the Genus *Scioena*" read by Lesueur on July 26, 1822. Concerning the latter, the editor of the *Philadelphia National Gazette and Literary Register* remarked: "Mr. Lesueur has here described three new species which the scientific ichthyologist refers to the Genus Scioena, but which our epicures will more readily recognise under its familiar name of Sheepshead. The number is embellished by a lithographical design of the fish, which exhibits, in an advantageous light, the state of this art among us."[78]   G. B.

Peter Guillet.
64 *Timber Merchant's Guide.* **Baltimore, Published by James Lovegrove, 1823.** American Antiquarian Society; gift of Charles H. Taylor, 1918.

The twenty-nine hand-colored plates, lithographed by Henry Stone of Washington, demonstrate the most efficient ways to saw trees to produce lumber. The book's introduction contains valuable information on forest management, the timber trade, and the selection of timber for maritime industries.   G. B.

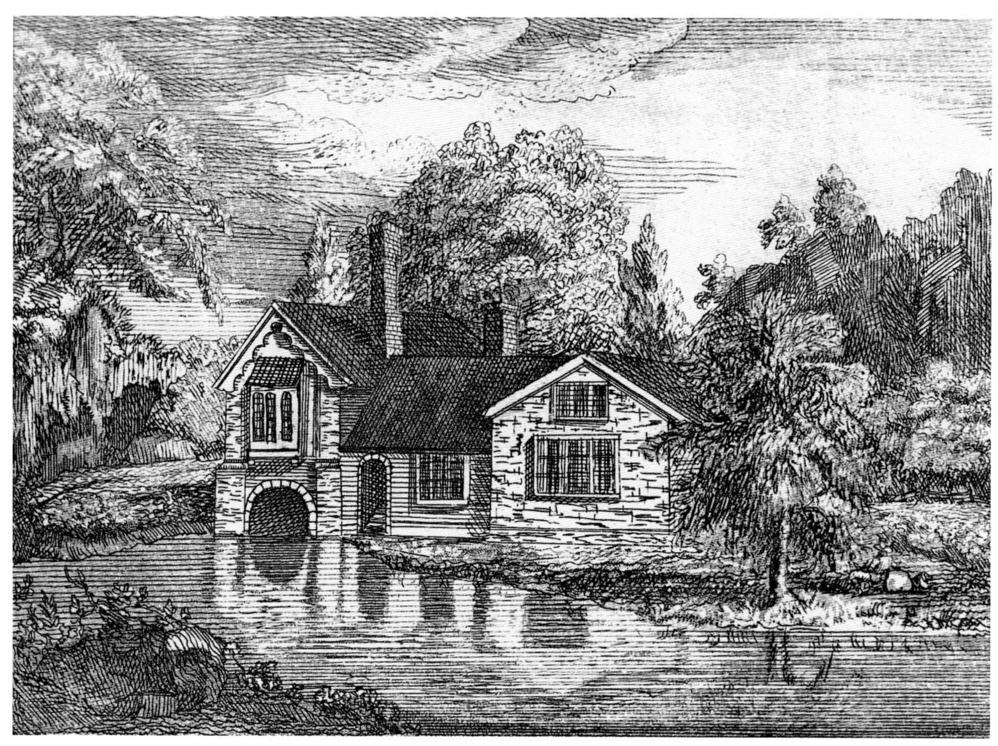

Cat. 60   Bass Otis, Plate from *Analectic Magazine* (1819).

65 *The Boston Monthly Magazine,* **vol. 1, December 1825. Boston, Printed by Ingraham & Hughes, 1825.**
Boston Athenæum; gift of Malcolm Johnson, 1977.

Three lithographs were printed as sample illustrations to accompany the article on lithography published in this issue. David Claypoole Johnston (1798–1865) provided a mill scene, Thomas Edwards (1795–1869) depicted another building by a body of water, and an anonymous artist drew a floral still life signed "Lithography of J. Pendleton." Only one lithograph was bound in each issue. The Boston Athenæum has numbers containing the flowers and Johnston's mill scene. The American Antiquarian Society has an extra-illustrated issue, a gift of Charles H. Taylor in 1928, containing all three lithographs.   S. P.

Cadwallader D. Colden (1769–1834).
66 *Memoir . . . Presented to the Mayor of the City, at the Celebration of the Completion of the New York Canals.* **New York, Printed by W. A. Davis, 1825.**
American Antiquarian Society; gift of Michael Papantonio, 1975.

The *Memoir* commemorates one of the great engineering accomplishments of the young American republic, the opening of the Erie Canal, connecting the Great Lakes to the Atlantic Ocean. The event was celebrated by a grand naval procession in New York Harbor on November 4, 1825; depictions of this parade and other festivities are recorded in this volume, which is also filled with maps, plans, and views detailing the canal's construction.

An appendix to the *Memoir* contains a history of lithography and its application to this important publication. The editor supplies information on the delineator of each of the fifty-five plates, thirty-six of which were printed by Anthony Imbert (1794/5–1834) in New York. Artists involved in the project in addition to Imbert were George Catlin (1796–1872), Abraham G. D. Tuthill (1776–1843), and Felix Duponchel (fl. 1825).   G. B.

Rembrandt Peale (1778–1860).
67 *Lithographic Sketches, Memoranda of Form and Character.* **No. 1. Boston, Published by Pendleton's Lithography, ca. 1827.**
Boston Athenæum; gift of Charles E. Mason, Jr., 1978.

Issued as a pamphlet with brown paper wrapper, this work consists of eight lithographic sketches mounted on pages with letterpress titles and captions. All were drawn

on stone by Rembrandt Peale and printed at Pendleton's Lithography, Boston. The Boston Athenæum collection contains two plates, *Anylayes Cherries* and *A Greek? No.* The complete pamphlet is in the collection of the American Antiquarian Society. (For an uncut sheet of the eight illustrations see Cat. 42). This is one of the works advertised for sale at the Peale Museum in Baltimore, run by Rembrandt's brother, Rubens Peale (1784–1865).   S. P.

John Rubens Smith (1775–1849).
68 *A Compendium of Picturesque Anatomy.* **Boston: Published by the author, 1827.**
American Antiquarian Society; John Thomas Lee Fund, 1981.

This book was presented to Gabriel Harrison (1818–1902), noted daguerreotypist and photographer.

The plates of this artists' anatomy book were drawn on stone by John Rubens Smith and printed by Pendleton's Lithography, Boston. In the Preface, Smith states that he adapted the plates from a work published in 1660 by Chrysostome Martinez, a Spanish artist and student in the College of Montaigu in France, to make up for the lack of available instruction manuals for artists. Smith's book carried endorsements from Washington Allston and Gilbert Stuart, both of whom cited the need of such a work among American students of the Fine Arts. This first number contains four plates and sold for $2.00; subsequent numbers of this projected three-part series were never published.   S. P.

69 *Spirit of the Old Dominion,* **vol. 1, no. 2. Richmond, Virginia, Published by Samuel Shepherd & Co., 1827.**
American Antiquarian Society.

The landscape view *Peaks of Otter, from Mr. A. B. Donald's Farm, Bedford, Va.,* was drawn by Harvey Mitchell (fl. 1827) and printed by John B. Martin (1797–1857) in Richmond. The indistinct quality of the impression, printed on pale pink paper, may be the result of using a local stone in place of imported lithographic stone. The back wrapper of this issue promised that each number of the *Spirit of the Old Dominion* would be illustrated with a lithograph by a native artist. Unfortunately, the magazine did not outlast the year.

The illustration accompanies an anonymous story, "The Rose of the Allegheny," which is set in the mountains of western Virginia. The twin "Peaks of Otter" are the source of the Otter River that traverses Virginia to the Atlantic. From the mid-1700s a road ran through the area

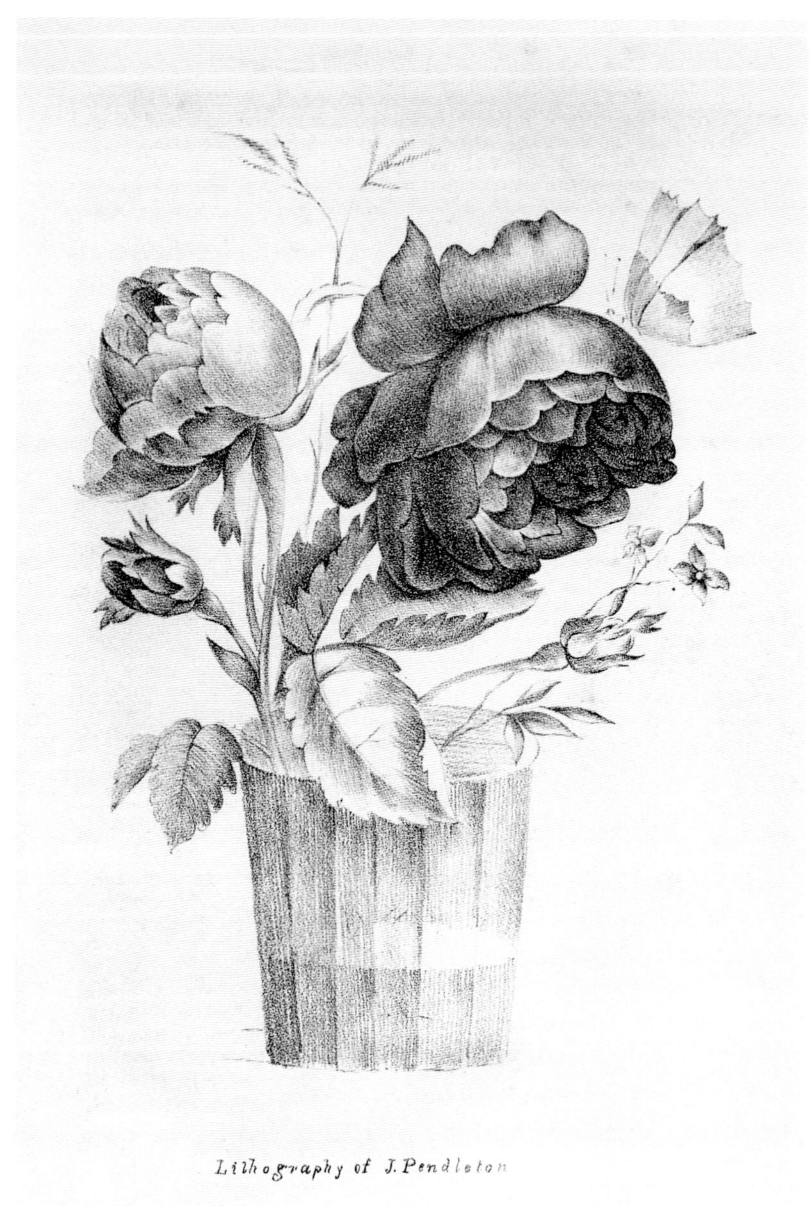

Cat. 65   John Pendleton, Plate from *Boston Monthly Magazine* (1825).

82

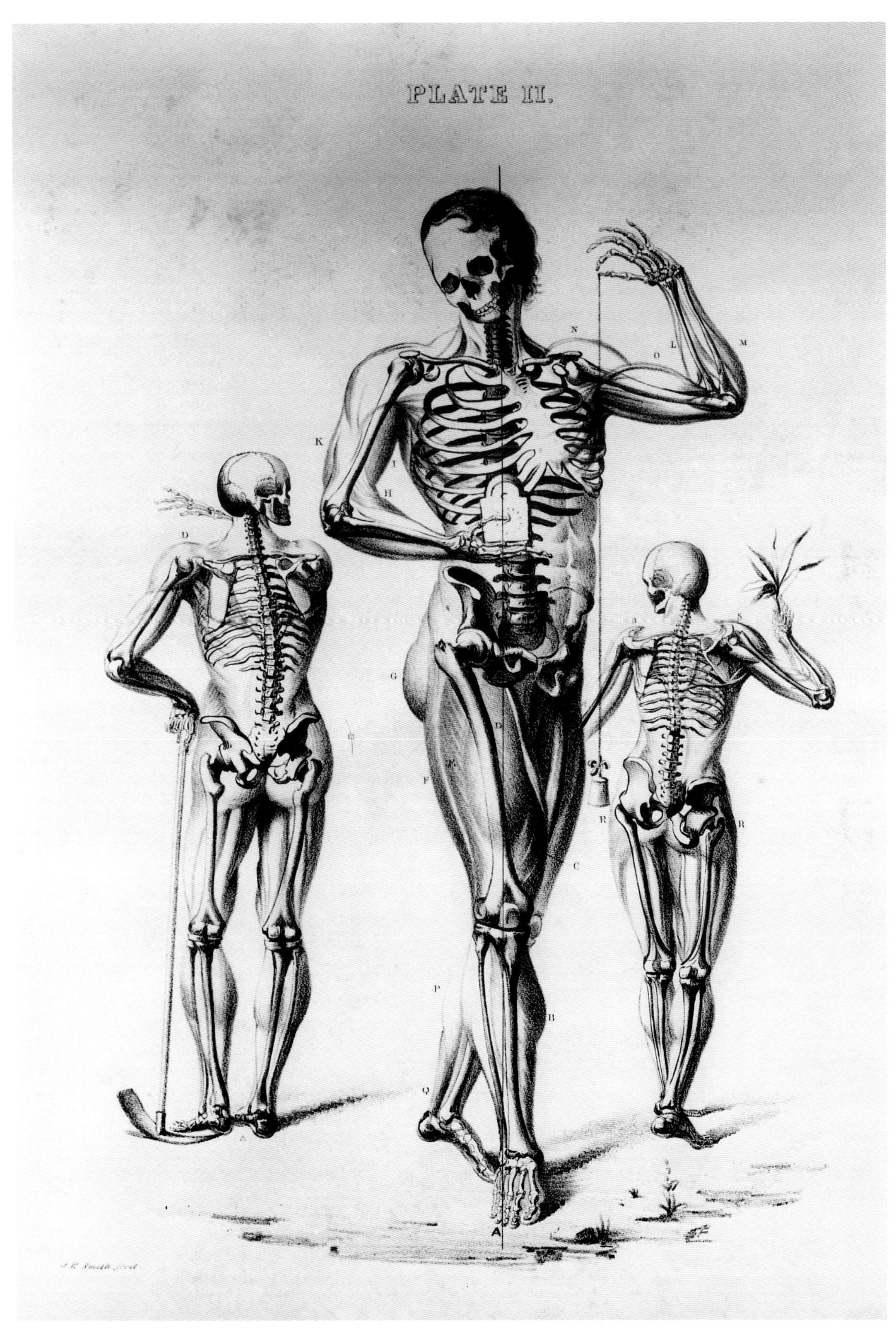

Cat. 68 John Rubens Smith, *Compendium of Picturesque Anatomy*, plate II (1827).

and by the early 1800s travelers could find accommodations in the vicinity of what is now a popular recreation area on the Blue Ridge Parkway.   G. B.

Charles Caldwell (1772–1853).

70 *A Discourse on the Genius and Character of the Rev. Horace Holley, L.L.D.* **Boston, Hilliard, Gray, Little, and Wilkins, 1828.**
Boston Athenæum; received May 28, 1835.

The lithograph of Lake Wonscopomac, signed "L. M.," was drawn by Louisa Davis Minot (1788–1858) and printed by Pendleton's Lithography, Boston. Minot was well acquainted with the Reverend Holley (1781–1827), and had stayed at his rural retreat on the shores of Lake Wonscopomac in Salisbury, Connecticut. Her view is included with a number of tributes to Holley, a Unitarian minister who assumed the presidency of Transylvania College at Lexington, Kentucky, in 1818. Under his popular leadership the college, and the medical school in particular, flourished; however, he was forced to resign in March 1827 because of his liberal religious views. His death, coming soon after, lent a partisan vehemence to this memorial volume, whose author, Charles Caldwell, was a professor at the Transylvania medical school.   G. B./S. P.

Anonymous.

71 *Phrenology.* **[Boston, 1829].**
American Antiquarian Society.

This small pamphlet in paper wrapper is one of the earliest American publications on phrenology, which is the study of the conformation of the skull to determine traits of character and mental aptitude. It was reviewed in the *Bower of Taste* for September 5, 1829. The editor writes: "*Phrenology.* A lithographic print has just been executed at the Senefelder press, from a drawing on stone by Mrs. Snow, a lady justly celebrated for her superior talents in this art. The print is well done and represents a front, back, and profile view of the human head; upon each of which are described the various compartments of the brain . . ."[79] Although expressing personal skepticism, the editor allows that "those who have a curiosity to look into the study of Phrenology, will find this publication a valuable assistant to their labors."[80]   S. P.

[Henry Thomas Alken] (1784–1851).

72 *The Beauties & Defects in the Figure of the Horse: Comparatively Delineated in a Series of Engravings.* **Boston, Published by Carter & Hendee, 1830.**
Boston Athenæum; gift of Charles E. Mason, Jr., 1977.

This book was adapted from one published in London in 1816, illustrated with color plates drawn by the author, and was conceived as a practical guide for riders, drivers, and purchasers of horses. It was also intended to be an instruction book for "such young Artists as are inclined to pursue the study of the Horse in all the different points of his figure and action." The plates address the fine points of equine anatomy and locomotion, several detailing the physiognomy of the horse as indicative of character and disposition. The frontispiece and title page of the Boston edition are pen lithographs, while the eighteen plates were drawn in the crayon manner. All were printed by Pendleton's Lithography, Boston.

The use of the word "engravings" on the title page rather than "lithographs" was typical of the period. Such usage may have stemmed from ignorance or a desire not to confuse the public, but may also reflect the prejudice that engravings were superior to lithographs.   S. P.

Jean-Gabriel Honoré Greppo (1788–1863).

73 *Essay on the Hieroglyphic System of M. Champollion, Jun. Translated from the French by Isaac Stuart.* **Boston, Perkins and Marvin, 1830.**
Boston Athenæum; gift of the publishers, 1831.

One of the important intellectual accomplishments of the early nineteenth century was Jean François Champollion's deciphering of Egyptian hieroglyphs using the Rosetta Stone. Moses Stuart, of the Andover Theological Seminary, underscores the importance of this milestone in his preface to Greppo's essay: "The great problem of Hieroglyphics is at last solved; and the veil has been lifted up which hid from past ages the mysteries that lay concealed under them." Popular interest was particularly engaged by the translation of inscriptions that substantiated historical events recounted in the Old Testament.

The two line illustrations in Greppo's book are elegant in their simplicity and clarity. Their style is reminiscent of copperplate engraving, but they were printed more economically by Pendleton's Lithography, Boston. Plate I reproduces cartouches containing the names of Ptolemy, Cleopatra, and the emperor Caesar; Plate II exhibits in columns three species of writing employed by the

Egyptians — the pure hieroglyphic, the hieratic, and the demotic — and compares these with the Roman alphabet.   G. B.

John C. Gunn.

74   *Gunn's Domestic Medicine, or Poor Man's Friend.*
**Knoxville, Tennessee, Published by the author,
1850.**
American Antiquarian Society; Michael Papantonio
Fund, 1986.

Addressing himself to simple families of the western and southern parts of the United States, John C. Gunn, himself a physician, set forth "in plain language, free from doctor's terms," common ailments and how they could be cured using local roots and herbs. The book was arranged "on a new and simple plan, by which the practice of medicine is reduced to principals of common sense." It seems completely appropriate that this book was dedicated to President Andrew Jackson, often scorned for his own radical notions of democracy.

The hand-colored frontispiece depicting the Greek myth of the origin of medicine was printed by Pendleton's Lithography, Boston, its classical theme reflecting the author's idealistic intentions.   S. P.

75   *The Ladies' Magazine,* **vol. 3, November 1850.
Boston, Published by John Putnam, 1850.**
Boston Athenæum.

As part of her crusade to improve American women, Sarah J. Hale (1788–1879), the editor of the *Ladies Magazine,* juxtaposed two dramatic images, both printed by Pendleton's Lithography, Boston. A hand-colored plate displaying extravagant *London & Parisian Fashions* faces a stark black and white image of two small children tugging at an old woman who has died in her chair before the fire. The reader is admonished: "Look here, upon this picture!" "And on this!" The accompanying articles amplify these themes. "The Fashions" admonishes American women not to follow "the whims and extravagances which prevail in the two most voluptuous and luxurious nations in the world of monarchies," urging them instead to adopt sensible and becoming styles "exhibiting republican taste" and fostering a native fashion industry. The story of "The Dying Grandmother" follows, a tale of a poor widow who has lost everything but her two grandchildren. Who will take care of them now that she is gone? It is an exhortation to benevolent activity.   S. P.

William Robert Prince (1795–1869), aided by
William Prince (1766–1842).

76   *A Treatise on the Vine; Embracing Its History
From the Earliest Ages to the Present Day.*
New York, Published by T. & J. Swords, et al., 1850.
Boston Athenæum; gift of D. J. Browne, 1831.

For the frontispiece to this work, William Prince drew the grape he had named and introduced into cultivation, *Vitis labrusca, v. Isabella.* His rendering was copied onto stone by Frederick Grain (fl. 1829–1857) and lithographed by Pendleton in New York. Both the Princes, father and son, were famous nurserymen, proprietors of the Linnaean Botanic Garden on Long Island.

Said to be a native of South Carolina, the Isabella grape was brought to New York State by Mrs. Isabella Gibbs, for whom it was named. Prince recommends this variety on economic grounds, stating: "There is no grape which will yield a greater quantity on a given space, or that can be made more lucrative in cultivation for the market than this kind. It also possesses the requisites to insure success in making wine of a fair quality, or for making brandy equal to that of France" (p. 166). Throughout the first half of the nineteenth century, the Isabella, along with the Catawba, was one of the most important American cultivars.   S. P.

Anonymous.

77   **Untitled [Composite figures printed by the
Senefelder Lithographic Company]. Boston,
Sold by T. Kettell, ca. 1830–1831.**
Boston Athenæum; gift of the New England
Historical Art Society, 1949.

This assembled album of eleven hand-colored lithographs has no title page or publication information. The prints were sold by Thomas Kettell, a Boston stationer and print seller who occupied the building at No. 59–61 Cornhill in December 1830, when the Senefelder Company moved there from their Washington Street address. A series of twelve figures, most of them identical to these, was also printed by Endicott & Swett in Baltimore and published there by J. N. Toy and W. R. Lucas in 1831. That set, also hand-colored, came in a paper wrapper bearing the title *Twelve Original Designs by G. Spratt.* The Baltimore set contains a plate entitled *Circulating Library,* that also exists as an engraving with the imprint of G. E. Madely, 3 Wellington Street, Strand (London), suggesting a British prototype for these unusual conceptions.[81]   S. P.

1. *Boston Directory* (Boston: Hunt & Simpson, 1825–1836). The partnership of Mitchell & Freeman apparently dissolved in 1831. The *Boston Directory* from 1832 to 1835 lists only "Freeman, Watson, crockery, 12 Chatman St." No listing of the store appears in the *Directory* after 1835.

2. Ellouise Baker Larsen, *American Historical Views on Staffordshire China* (New York: Doubleday, Doran & Co., 1939), 141–142.

3. John Carbonell, "Anthony Imbert: New York's Pioneer Lithographer," in *Prints and Printmakers of New York State, 1825–1940,* ed. David Tatham (Syracuse, NY: Syracuse University Press, 1986), 21–22; fig. 1.3.

4. Quoted in Howard Thomas, *Trenton Falls Yesterday and Today* (New York: Prospect Books, 1951), 21.

5. W. S. Tyler, *History of Amherst College During Its First Half Century* (Springfield, MA.: Clark W. Bryan and Co., 1873), 657.

6. Gloria Gilda Deak, *Picturing America 1497–1899.* 2 v. (Princeton NJ: Princeton University Press, 1988), 1:243, 2:359.

7. Edward Hitchcock, *Reminiscences of Amherst College* (Northampton, MA.: Bridgman & Childs, 1863), 56.

8. *Obituary Record of Graduates of Amherst College for the Academical Year Ending July 8, 1875* (Amherst, MA.: Henry McCloud, 1875), 52–53.

9. Quoted in Margaret E. White, ed., *A Sketch of Chester Harding, Artist Drawn by His Own Hand* (Boston: Houghton, Mifflin and Co., 1890), 187n.

10. Quoted in Leah Lipton, *Family Connections: Portraits by Chester Harding* (Framingham, MA.: Danforth Museum, 1981), 5.

11. William Ellery Channing, "Remarks on the Life and Character of Napoleon Bonaparte," in *Discourses, Reviews, and Miscellanies* (Boston: Carter and Hendee, 1830), 159.

12. *Art Journal,* n.s. 4 (June 1865), 191. See also *Art Journal,* n.s. 5 (March 1859), 73–75.

13. Carbonell, "Anthony Imbert," 34; fig. 1.7.

14. Quoted in Nicholas B. Wainwright, *Philadelphia in the Romantic Age of Lithography* (Philadelphia: Historical Society of Pennsylvania, 1958), 14.

15. James Thompson, *Discourse Delivered in Salem, September 9, 1849, as a Tribute to the Memory of Rev. Henry Colman* (Boston: Wm. Crosby & H. P. Nichols, 1849), 11–15.

16. Eliza Susan Quincy, *Scrapbooks* (1830–1836), 7:119. According to Bettina A. Norton, an impression in the Essex Institute has a hand-written inscription attributing the print to J. F. Colman.

17. Bettina A. Norton, *Prints at the Essex Institute* (Salem, MA.: Essex Institute, 1978), 49–50.

18. Josiah Quincy, *A Municipal History of the Town and City of Boston* (Boston: Charles C. Little and James Brown, 1852), 75.

19. Quincy, 383–384.

20. *National Academy of Design Exhibition Record 1826–1860.* 2 v. (New York: New York Historical Society, 1943), 1: 114.

21. William Dunlap, *History of the Rise and Progress of the Arts and Design in the United States.* 2 v. (New York: George P. Scott and Co., 1834), 2:409–10.

22. Julia D. Sophronia Snow, "Delineators of the Adams-Jackson American Views," *Antiques,* 31 (January 1937): 26–28.

23. William Bentley, *Diary of William Bentley, D. D.* 4 v. (Salem, MA.: Essex Institute, 1907), 2:317.

24. Fiske Kimball, *Mr. Samuel McIntire, Carver: The Architect of Salem* (Portland, ME.: Southworth-Anthoensen Press, 1940), 63–65; figs. 57–65.

25. Hannah Josephson, *The Golden Threads: New England's Mill Girls and Magnates* (New York: Russell & Russell, 1967), 221, 230–231, 240–41.

26. Hannah Kinney, *A Review of the Principal Events of the Last Ten Years in the Life of Mrs. Hannah Kinney: Together with Some Comments upon the Late Trial* (Boston: J. N. Bradley & Co., 1841), 26–28.

27. *Columbian Centinel,* September 23, 1835, p. 2, col. 2.

28. Charles Cowley, *Illustrated History of Lowell,* rev. ed. (Boston: Lee & Shepard, 1868), 87, 111–113.

29. *Trial of Mrs. Hannah Kinney for the Alleged Murder of Her Husband, George T. Kinney by Poison* (Boston: Times and Notion Office, 1840), 9–10.

30. *Outline of the System of Education at the Round Hill School* (Boston, 1831), 4.

31. George Bancroft and Joseph Green Cogswell, *Prospectus of a School to be Established at Round Hill, Northampton, Massachusetts* (Cambridge, MA.: University Press, 1823), 3.

32. Bancroft and Cogswell, 18.

33. Robert Hale Newton, *Town and Davis Architects* (New York: Columbia University Press, 1942), 51–52, 93.

34. John Spencer Bassett, "The Round Hill School," in *Proceedings of the American Antiquarian Society,* n.s. 27 (1917), 47–48.

35. Stephen D. Stephens, *The Mavericks* (New Brunswick, NJ.: Rutgers University Press, 1950), 183–184.

36. John Sullivan, "The Case of 'A Late Student': Pictorial Satire in Jacksonian America," in *Proceedings of the American Antiquarian Society,* 83 (October 1973), 277–286.

37. Franz Ludwig Jahn, *Treatise on Gymnasticks,* trans. Charles Beck (Northampton, MA. Simeon Butler, 1828), iv.

38. *Columbian Centinel,* July 29, 1826, p. 1.

39. Ibid.

40. David F. Tatham, "David Claypoole Johnston's Theatrical Portraits," in *American Portrait Prints,* ed. Wendy Wick Reaves (Washington, DC.: National Portrait Gallery, 1984), 162–193.

41. *Columbian Centinel,* September 23, 1826, p. 2, col. 3.

42. Louis P. Hager and Albert D. Handy, eds., *History of the Old Colony Railroad* (Boston: Hager and Handy, 1893), 14–15, 20, 87.

43. Steve Dunwell, *The Run of the Mill* (Boston: David Godine, 1978), 27.

44. Quoted in Daniel Munro Wilson, *Three Hundred Years of Quincy, 1625–1925* (Boston: Wright & Potter, 1926), 39.

45. Quoted in Mabel M. Swan, "The American Kings" *Antiques,* 19 (April 1931), 281.

46. Ibid.

47. Ibid.

48. D. E. Williams, *The Life and Correspondence of Sir Thomas Lawrence, Kt.* (London: Henry Colburn and Richard Bentley, 1831), 342, 345.

49. Williams, 337–338.

50. Katharine Minot Channing, ed., *Minot Family Letters 1773–1871* (Sherborn, MA.: 1957), 252.

51. Channing, ed., 263.

52. John A. Mahey, "Lithographs of Rembrandt Peale," *Antiques,* 97 (February 1970), 239.

53. C. Edwards Lester, *The Artists of America* (New York: Baker & Scribner, 1846), 216.

54. *North American Review,* 20 (January 1825), 45.

55. Lester, 204.

56. Lester, 210.

57. Ibid.

58. Martha Chadbourne Kettelle, *Aloft on Butterflies' Wings: The Story of the Artist Charles Henry Granger and His Family* (Paoli, PA.: Daylesford Abbey Printing, 1976), 20–21.

59. Lester, 210.

60. Lester, 211.

61. Dunlap, 2:57n.

62. *The Franklin Journal and American Mechanics Magazine,* 4 (1827), 403.

63. Dunlap, 2:57n.

64. Quoted in Carol Eaton Hevner, "The Paintings of Rembrandt Peale: Character and Convention," in Lillian B. Miller, *In Pursuit of Fame: Rembrandt Peale 1778–1860* (Washington, DC.: National Portrait Gallery, Smithsonian Institute, 1992), 280.

65. I am indebted to Rona Schneider for this information.

66. *The National Gazette and Literary Register,* October 18, 1826, p. 1.

67. Godefroy Engelmann, *Manuel du dessinateur lithographe* (Paris, 1822), 45.

68. William R. Staples, *Annals of the Town of Providence* (Providence, RI.: Knowles and Vose, 1843), 633–634.

69. *An Appendix Containing the Act of Incorporation of the Humane Society of the Commonwealth of Massachusetts…* (Boston, 1791), 17–18.

70. *An Appendix,* 23.

71. *An Appendix,* 24.

72. *History of the Humane Society of the Commonwealth of Massachusetts* (Boston: T. R. Marvin & Son, 1877), 40.

73. *History of the Humane Society of Massachusetts: With a Selected List of Premiums* (Boston: Samuel N. Dickinson, 1845), 50–51.

74. *Boston Daily Advertiser,* July 30, 1830, p. 1., col. 6.

75. "Mr. I. Jone's [sic] Benefit — A Card," *Columbian Centinel,* March 24, 1830, p. 3, col. 4.

76. "Mr. Peile's Concert," *Columbian Centinel,* April 3, 1830, p. 2, col. 3.

77. Stephen Nissenbaum, *The Battle for Christmas* (New York: Alfred A. Knopf, 1996), 71–76.

78. August 27, 1822, p. 2; editor's review.

79. P. 576.

80. Ibid.

81. *Twelve Original Designs by G. Spratt* is in the American Antiquarian Society collection, as is the British engraving of the *Circulating Library,* located in Joel Munsell's scrapbook in the manuscript collection.